How We Got the
Book of Mormon

HOW WE GOT THE
BOOK OF MORMON

RICHARD E. TURLEY JR.
WILLIAM W. SLAUGHTER

DESERET
BOOK

Salt Lake City, Utah

Unless noted below, all photographs or images are courtesy of the Church History Library, The Church of Jesus Christ of Latter-day Saints. Used by permission.

Page x: *Mormon Abridging the Plates,* by Tom Lovell. © Intellectual Reserve, Inc.

Page xv: *Moroni Hides the Plates in the Hill Cumorah,* by Tom Lovell. © Intellectual Reserve, Inc.

Page 6: Photograph of golden plates replica by Steve Bunderson.

Page 45: Image of printer's manuscript; courtesy of Community of Christ.

Page 52: Panorama of Cincinnati waterfront; 1848 daguerreotype by Charles Fontayne and William Porter. Courtesy of Public Library of Cincinnati and Hamilton County, Ohio.

Page 56: Photograph of Ebenezer Robinson; courtesy of Community of Christ.

Page 63: Cornerstone of the Nauvoo House, photograph by George Edward Anderson; courtesy of Harold B. Lee Library, Brigham Young University.

Page 66: Detail of *Herefordshire Beacon,* by Al Rounds. © Al Rounds; available at www.alrounds.com.

Page 80: Detail of *Port of Liverpool,* circa 1840. Steel engraving by J. Godfrey, based on a painting by C. H. Cox. Courtesy of Liverpool History Society.

© 2011 Richard E. Turley Jr. and William W. Slaughter

All rights reserved. No part of this book may be reproduced in any form or by any means without permission in writing from the publisher, Deseret Book Company, P. O. Box 30178, Salt Lake City, Utah 84130. This work is not an official publication of The Church of Jesus Christ of Latter-day Saints. The views expressed herein are the responsibility of the authors and do not necessarily represent the position of the Church or of Deseret Book Company.

DESERET BOOK is a registered trademark of Deseret Book Company.

Visit us at DeseretBook.com

Library of Congress Cataloging-in-Publication Data
Turley, Richard E. (Richard Eyring), 1956– author.
  How we got the Book of Mormon / Richard E. Turley, Jr., William W. Slaughter.
     pages cm
  Includes bibliographical references and index.
  ISBN 978-1-60908-062-4 (hardbound : alk. paper)
  1. Book of Mormon—History. I. Slaughter, William W., 1952– author. II. Title.
BX8627.T83 2011
298.3'22—dc23   2011016377

Printed in the United States of America
Worzalla Publishing Co., Stevens Point, WI

10 9 8 7 6 5 4 3 2 1

Contents

Preface vii
Prologue xi
1. THE GOLDEN PLATES 1
2. THE TRANSLATION 13
3. THE FIRST EDITION, 1830 27
4. THE SECOND EDITION, 1837 39
5. THE THIRD EDITION, 1840 53
6. THE FIRST EUROPEAN EDITION, 1841 67
7. CHAPTER AND VERSE 81
8. THE 1920 EDITION 93
9. THE 1981 EDITION 107
10. "THE KEYSTONE OF OUR RELIGION" 117
Notes 129
Index 151

Preface

We have written this book to help members of The Church of Jesus Christ of Latter-day Saints better understand the history of the Book of Mormon, a work revered as scripture by the Church's members. Some 150 million copies of the Book of Mormon have been printed in more than 100 languages, reflecting the book's growing worldwide influence.[1] Readers can verify the facts in our book by consulting the sources cited in the notes, which we have deliberately tucked in the back so as not to interrupt our narrative.

Our book also contains stories or statements of belief that will be familiar to Latter-day Saints but may seem new or foreign to others. To the latter, we recommend Samuel Taylor Coleridge's widely recognized admonition to adopt "that willing suspension of disbelief for the moment, which constitutes poetic faith."[2] Or, as a Book of Mormon prophet put it, "experiment upon my words, and exercise a particle of faith."[3] Doing so will help them better understand what Latter-day Saints believe.

Although we cite scholarly sources, we intend this book for general readers and have followed widely accepted editing practices aimed at ease of reading. For example, we have modernized spelling, punctuation, and capitalization.

We wish to thank the many people who helped make this book a reality. Our book designer, Sheryl Dickert, spent long hours with us, helping to integrate the text and visuals. Matthew Reier took excellent photographs.

At Deseret Book, Sheri Dew, Cory Maxwell, Anne Sheffield, and Richard Erickson encouraged our work from the beginning.

Our colleagues in the Church History Department of The Church of Jesus Christ of Latter-day Saints, at Brigham Young University, and elsewhere provided help and suggestions. Glenn Rowe was endlessly patient in providing access to rare materials. April Williamsen facilitated image and document scanning. Peter Crawley, Matthew J. Grow, Reid L. Neilson, Eric C. Olson, and Royal Skousen provided peer review. Elders Russell M. Nelson, Jeffrey R. Holland, and Marlin K. Jensen generously offered their insights, although we alone are responsible for the volume's final contents.

Finally, we wish to thank our families, especially our wives—Shirley Swensen Turley and Sheri E. Slaughter—for their help, support, and patience.

We hope readers find the book interesting, informative, and inspiring.

The prophet Mormon.

Prologue

In A.D. 321, civil unrest reigned among people in the Americas. A gang of thieves—the Gadianton robbers—spread across the land, wreaking havoc. Parasites on society, they lived on the labors of others by killing, enslaving, or driving them off and consuming the work of their hands. In time, they would destroy all who would not accept their evil ways and bow to their demands.[1]

The Gadiantons reveled in gold and silver and sought to destroy the sacred records of the Christians, the people who accepted and tried to live the gospel of Jesus Christ. These records inscribed on metal plates had been passed down from generation to generation to preserve the sacred history of the people. Without such records, their faith and language would become corrupted.[2]

In that year of 321, Ammaron, keeper of the records of this Christian people, sensed growing danger and concealed the sacred engravings in a hill, entrusting them to the Lord. Knowing the promises contained in the records, he believed they would someday come forth to bless those who survived the coming devastation.[3]

Perhaps he would be the last to see the sacred writings in his lifetime. Or perhaps there would be another.

There was another. Not long after hiding the records, Ammaron noticed a ten-year-old boy who stood out from others. The boy had a revered name—Mormon—the name of his own father, the name of the land where his people had regained their spirituality after wallowing for an era in sin.[4]

At age ten, Mormon had already become, as he himself put it, "learned somewhat after the manner of the learning of my people."

Ammaron approached him. "I perceive that thou art a sober child, and art quick to observe," Ammaron said. "Therefore, when ye are about twenty and four years old I would that ye should remember the things that ye have observed concerning this people."[5]

At that time—fourteen years in the future—Ammaron wanted Mormon to go to the hill where the records were stored and take a set of metal plates made by Mormon's forefather Nephi. Leave the other records where they are, Ammaron instructed, and write on the plates of Nephi what you have observed about the people.

"I remembered the things which Ammaron commanded me," Mormon later wrote. Meanwhile, he kept mental notes on the declining state of his people.[6]

At age eleven, Mormon went south with his father to the land of Zarahemla. "The whole face of the land had become covered with buildings," he observed, "and the people were as numerous almost, as it were the sand of the sea." That year, war broke out on the outskirts of Zarahemla by the river Sidon. Mormon's people won, but the peace lasted only four years.[7]

The people grew wicked, and the miracles and healings that once characterized their times ceased. But Mormon stayed worthy, and at age fifteen, near the end of the period of peace, he met the Savior face to face. "I was visited of the Lord," Mormon wrote, "and tasted and knew of the goodness of Jesus."[8]

God forbade him from preaching to the people because they had willfully rebelled. As a silent witness, Mormon watched the Gadiantons infest the land. He saw prophecy fulfilled as the people rejected true religion for sorceries, witchcraft, and magic.[9]

When war broke out again, Mormon's people begged him to lead them. Like his ancestor Nephi, he was "large in stature" despite his youth. At age fifteen, Mormon took charge of an army and entered the war, hoping to save his people.[10]

As the conflict wore on, "blood and carnage spread throughout all the face of the land." Seeing the destruction, his people mourned, and Mormon felt hopeful that they would turn to God for deliverance.[11]

"But behold," Mormon wrote, "this my joy was vain, for their sorrowing was not unto repentance, because of the goodness of God; but it was rather the sorrowing of the damned, because the Lord would not always suffer them to take happiness in sin." Instead of turning to Jesus "with broken hearts and contrite spirits, . . . they did curse God, and wish to die." Even then, "they would struggle with the sword for their lives" when threatened.[12]

Around A.D. 335, when Mormon was twenty-four, he went as instructed by Ammaron and removed the plates of Nephi from the hill repository. On them, he began keeping a detailed record of his people's decline.[13]

Over the next five decades, Mormon preached repentance to his people, led them in battle, and did everything else he could to save them. But they would not be saved.[14]

Finally, in A.D. 385, when Mormon was in his mid-seventies, he gathered his people together for one final battle near a hill called Cumorah. God had commanded him not to let the sacred records "fall into the hands" of enemies who "would destroy them." "Knowing it to be the last struggle of my people," wrote Mormon, "I . . . hid up in the hill Cumorah all the records . . . save it were these few plates which I gave unto my son Moroni."[15] (Mormon likely named his son Moroni after a heroic military leader, one of the sterling characters he had discovered while abridging the sacred records.)[16]

Like his father, Mormon, Moroni commanded ten thousand people in the final battle at Cumorah, as did each of twenty-one other leaders in their army. Nearly a quarter million of their people watched in horror as the enemy approached with far greater numbers. "They did fall upon my people with the sword, and with the bow, and with the arrow, and with the ax, and with all manner of weapons of war," agonized Mormon, who survived to the next morning with just twenty-four others of his people, including Moroni.[17]

But the killing did not end. By A.D. 401, the enemy had tracked down the survivors and destroyed nearly all of them. "My father also was killed by them," wrote Moroni on golden plates, "and I even remain alone to write the sad tale of the destruction of my people."[18]

Moroni escaped death for some twenty more years before hiding up the golden plates for future generations to discover.[19]

During those years, he added to the record. One addition was an abridged account of the Jaredites, a people who had lived in the Americas for hundreds of years before Moroni's civilization. Moroni had access to their record and to two stones used to interpret languages. Knowing the old languages would become extinct, Moroni buried the interpreters with the plates.[20]

Before sealing up the golden record, Moroni prophesied: "It shall be brought out of darkness unto light, according to the word of God; yea, it shall be brought out of the earth, and it shall shine forth out of darkness, and come unto the knowledge of the people; and it shall be done by the power of God.... For the eternal purposes of the Lord shall roll on, until all his promises shall be fulfilled."[21]

The prophet Moroni.

The Hill Cumorah, where the golden plates were found.

Chapter One
THE GOLDEN PLATES

On September 22, 1823, seventeen-year-old American farm boy Joseph Smith went to the tallest hill near his home in upstate New York. He was led there by the instructions of an angel who had visited him three times in his bedroom the night before and a fourth time that morning near a field where Joseph had been working with his father and brothers.[1]

On the west side of the hill near the top, he found a large stone. Prying it up, he peered down into a stone box. Inside, on a platform of crossways rocks, lay a stack of golden metal plates or sheets, linked with three rings into a book. Beside them lay two stones in silver bows like old-fashioned spectacles.[2]

The angel had told him the purpose of the plates was to glorify God, not to get rich. But Joseph and his family were poor. They were struggling to buy their own farm and needed all the money they could get. Maybe, Joseph thought, there was something in the box they could use. He reached in, only to be thrown back by a sudden shock.[3]

Moroni—the angel Joseph had seen in his recent visions—appeared again, forbidding him to take the objects just yet. Joseph needed training first to assure

Moroni delivers the golden plates to Joseph Smith in 1827.

that he would see them as sacred to God's purposes, not as treasures to be used for worldly gain.[4]

Four years later to the day, not long after midnight, a more mature Joseph returned to the hill in a borrowed wagon, his new bride, Emma, at his side. She waited below while he retrieved the plates. Moroni delivered them with a charge: "That I should be responsible for them," Joseph wrote, "that if I should let them go carelessly, or through any neglect of mine, I should be cut off; but that if I would use all my endeavors to preserve them, until he, the messenger, should call for them, they should be protected."[5]

Characters from the golden plates.

Joseph kept the plates less than two years before returning them to Moroni.[6] During that time, he came to know the ancient records well. "These records were engraven on plates which had the appearance of gold," he wrote in 1842. "Each plate was six inches wide and eight inches long and not quite so thick as common tin."[7]

"They were filled with engravings, in Egyptian characters and bound together in a volume, as the leaves of a book with three rings running through the whole," he said. "The volume was something near six inches in thickness, a part of which was sealed."[8]

A friend of the Smiths, a respectable farmer named Martin Harris, saw the plates. He thought the rings were silver and that the whole record weighed forty or fifty pounds. Another friend, David Whitmer, who also saw the ancient record, said the sealed portion made up half or two-thirds of the volume.[9]

Emma never saw the plates without their being wrapped in linen cloth. But they often sat on a table where the Smiths lived, and she moved them around as she did housework. "I once felt of the plates, as they thus lay on the table, tracing their outline and shape," she told an interested listener. "They seemed to be pliable like thick paper, and would rustle with a metallic sound when the edges were moved by the thumb."[10]

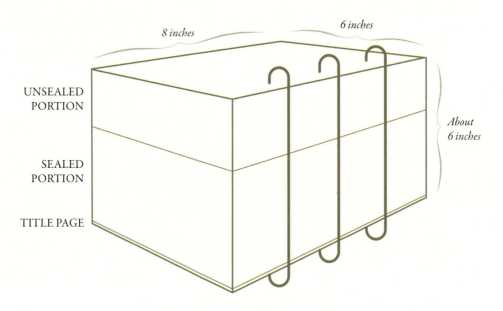

The golden plates, as described by Joseph Smith.

Emma Hale Smith, wife of Joseph Smith, said the pages of the golden plates were pliable like thick paper.

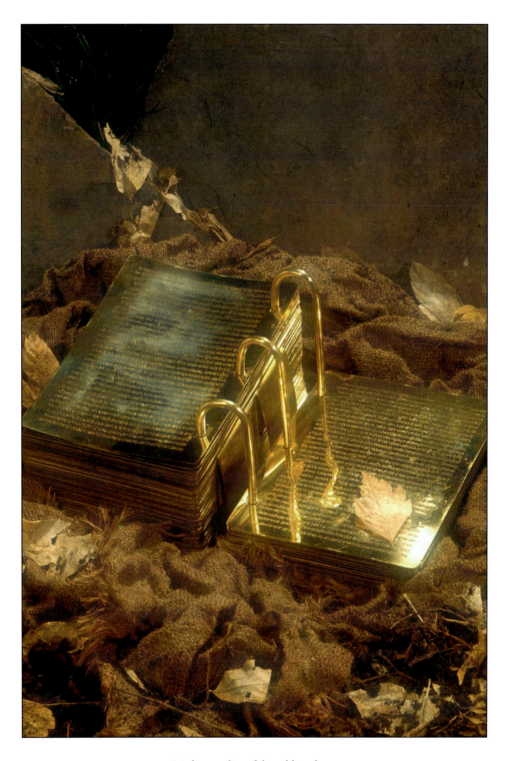

Modern replica of the golden plates.

THE GOLDEN PLATES

The "reformed Egyptian" language of the plates had both Egyptian and Hebrew traits.[11] In 1839, Joseph said that wording for the record's title page came from "the very last leaf, on the left hand side of the collection or book of plates . . . the language of the whole running same as all Hebrew writing in general."[12] Hebrew runs right to left, as Joseph knew from his study of the language.[13] That likely meant the rings binding the volume were on the righthand side as it sat upright.

LARGE PLATES OF NEPHI

Mormon's Abridgment and Own Writings
Lehi   Mosiah   Alma   Helaman   3 Nephi   4 Nephi   Mormon 1–7

Moroni's Abridgment and Own Writings
Mormon 8–9   Ether   Moroni

SMALL PLATES OF NEPHI
1 Nephi   2 Nephi   Jacob   Enos   Jarom   Omni

WORDS OF MORMON *Written by Mormon*

SEALED PORTION
Added by Moroni

TITLE PAGE *Written by Moroni*

Although no one today knows exactly how the records on the golden plates were arranged, this figure offers one possibility based on reasonable assumptions.

The unsealed part of the plates contained two major sets of records: the plates of Mormon and the small plates of Nephi. Anciently, Moroni's father, Mormon, abridged a detailed chronicle of his people—the large plates of Nephi—into a smaller record: the plates of Mormon. He then bound in with them the small plates of Nephi, an unabridged record that covered part of the same time period but focused on spiritual matters.[14]

Before Mormon died in battle, he gave this combined set of plates to Moroni, who engraved on them an abridged account of the Jaredites, the people who had preceded the Nephites in the Western Hemisphere but had become extinct. Moroni added his own history and reflections before burying the plates where Joseph found them.[15]

The sealed portion of the plates came from a record made by the first Jaredite prophet, who was known as "the brother of Jared."[16] Because Moroni abridged this record, he knew its contents and referred to them in his writings. Other prophets did the same.[17]

According to Moroni, the brother of Jared saw the premortal Christ face-to-face on a high mountain.[18] During the vision, the Lord showed him "all the inhabitants of the earth which had been, and also all that would be."[19] This was "a revelation from God, from the beginning of the world to the ending thereof."[20]

The Lord commanded the brother of Jared to write the vision and seal it up; it would not be made public until after His crucifixion.[21] To assure the vision's sanctity, it was written in the language of Adam, which later people would be unable to read without "two stones" given to the brother of Jared. He was to seal them up with the record, and "in my own due time," the Lord said, "these stones shall magnify to the eyes of men these things which ye shall write."[22]

When Christ died in the Old World, "terrible destruction" ravaged the Americas.[23] Many wicked people perished, and after nearly a year's time—which offered space for repentance—Christ appeared to the penitent gathered at a temple in a land called Bountiful.[24] A long period of righteousness ensued, during which the vision of the brother of Jared was revealed once more.[25]

After the people grew wicked again, Moroni wrote the vision on the golden plates and sealed that portion of them, burying with them the interpreter stones.[26] When Joseph got the plates, he also received the very stones passed down from the brother of Jared.[27]

The title page for the golden plates called the entire compilation "The Book of Mormon," declaring that it was "written by the hand of Mormon" and "sealed by the hand of Moroni."[28]

Each section of the golden plates points future readers to Jesus Christ. "My prayer to God is concerning my brethren, that they may once again come to the knowledge of God, yea, the redemption of Christ," wrote Mormon as he was about to deliver his record to his son Moroni.[29]

In writing what he thought would be his last words on the plates, Moroni bade "farewell" to future readers "until we shall meet before the judgment-seat of Christ," where all would know of a surety "that I have seen Jesus, and that he hath talked with me face to face." Moroni invited all "to seek this Jesus of whom the prophets and apostles have written."[30]

When he unexpectedly had a chance to write again, Moroni renewed his invitation. "Yea, come unto Christ, and be perfected in him, and deny yourselves of all ungodliness," he urged, that "through the shedding of the blood of Christ . . . unto the remission of your sins, . . . ye become holy, without spot."[31]

Finally, the title page, inscribed by Moroni before burying the plates, said their purpose was to convince others "that Jesus is the Christ, the Eternal God, manifesting Himself unto all nations."[32]

No wonder that more than a century and a half after Joseph received the golden plates from the angel Moroni, millions would accept the record as "another testament of Jesus Christ."[33]

But that could not happen until after the plates had been translated by Joseph Smith, dictated to scribes, and published to the world as scripture.

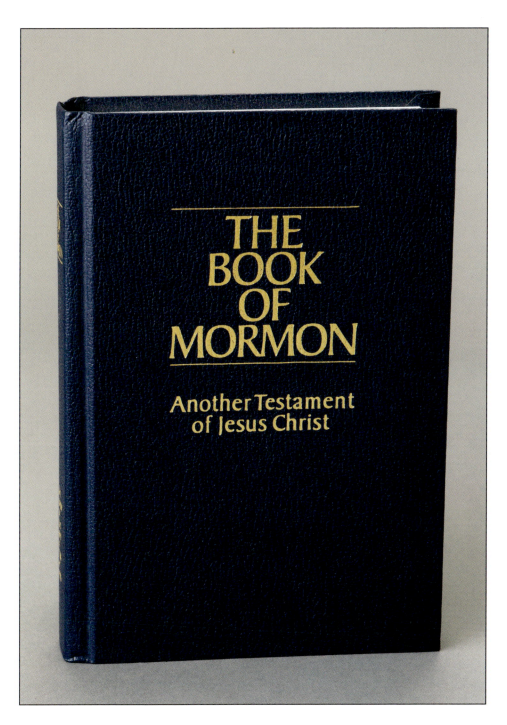

Millions today accept the Book of Mormon as another testament of Jesus Christ.

The center structure was the home of Joseph and Emma Smith in Harmony, Pennsylvania, where much of the Book of Mormon was translated. The structures on either side were added later.

Chapter Two
THE TRANSLATION

After Joseph Smith received the plates from Moroni, persecution drove him and Emma to her parents' neighborhood in Harmony, Pennsylvania. Martin Harris gave the young couple fifty dollars to help them move. To protect the plates, Joseph hid them in a barrel of beans during the 140-mile journey.[1]

When Joseph got to Pennsylvania in December 1827, he copied some characters from the plates and translated part of them. In February 1828, he gave a sheet of his work to Martin Harris, who took it to New York and showed it to scholars. Martin told one linguist that some of the plates were sealed. "I cannot read a sealed book," the professor scoffed. In April, Martin returned to Harmony, convinced he should serve as scribe while Joseph dictated the translation of the golden record.[2]

During the time Joseph had the plates, several people watched him translate. They said that rather than looking at the record itself, he looked into the interpreters or another seer stone, blocking out external light, such as by placing the interpreters in his hat and putting his face down into it.[3] Joseph himself, however, refused to elaborate on a process he considered sacred. He "said that it was not intended to tell the world all the particulars of the coming forth of the Book of Mormon."[4] He said simply that he translated "by the gift and power of God."[5]

In short, the translation came by revelation. Joseph could not read the language on the golden plates by himself. He needed God's help. With that help, he could translate, even if he wasn't looking directly at the record. In a similar way a year later, Joseph and a scribe translated another ancient document, a "parchment, written and hid up" by Christ's apostle John, "the beloved disciple." That translation too came as a revelation; Joseph did not suggest the document was even in the Western Hemisphere when it was translated.[6]

Martin arrived in Harmony around April 12, 1828, to act as Joseph's scribe for the golden plates translation. By June 14, the men had filled 116 manuscript pages with a translation of the book of Lehi and perhaps part of the book of Mosiah. Soon, Joseph wrote, Martin "began to tease me to give him liberty to carry the writings home and shew them" to people there. Martin hoped to "convince them of the truth."[7]

Joseph prayed to know if Martin should take the pages. The Lord told Joseph "he must not." Martin "was not satisfied." Joseph asked again and received the same answer. Martin "could not be contented" and begged Joseph to ask one more time. Joseph finally asked again, and this time "permission was granted," provided Martin showed the pages to only five named family members.[8]

On June 15, after Martin had left for New York, Joseph's wife, Emma, gave birth to their first child. The newborn son soon died, and Emma "seemed, for some time, more like sinking with her infant into the mansion of the dead, than remaining with her husband among the living."[9]

*Joseph and Emma Smith lost their first child soon after
Martin Harris left for New York with the 116 manuscript pages.*

For two weeks, "Joseph slept not an hour in undisturbed quiet" as he cared for Emma. When she finally began to mend, "another cause of trouble forced itself upon his mind." Martin had been gone almost three weeks, and Joseph had heard nothing from him. Things were not going the way they had agreed.

Joseph didn't want to agitate Emma as she healed and said nothing to her about his worries. A few days later, however, she asked him to get her mother to care for her so he could go to Palmyra and figure out what was wrong.[10]

Joseph caught the first stagecoach toward Palmyra and had time to think as he rode along. He knew that if Martin had lost the pages, he, Joseph, could not recover the translation without God's help. And that "was something Joseph could hardly hope for" because, "by persisting in his entreaties to the Lord," he may have sinned. Despite utter exhaustion, "sleep fled from his eyes, neither had he any desire for food, for he felt that he had done wrong, and how great his condemnation was he did not know."[11]

Just one other passenger rode in the stage, and the stranger asked Joseph what was wrong. Joseph talked of his dead child and sick wife but said nothing more until they reached their stop. By then it was 10:00 p.m., and Joseph remarked he had twenty miles still to go on foot. The stranger noticed Joseph hadn't slept or eaten since they started the trip. He was worried Joseph would fall asleep in the woods, "meeting with some awful disaster."[12]

He volunteered to accompany Joseph and walked all night with him to Joseph's parents' house. The last four miles of the trip, the stranger had to lead Joseph by the arm because he was so worn out that he kept falling asleep. When they got to the Smith home, the man told Joseph's parents their son was sick and needed rest and nourishment.

After Joseph had something to eat, he asked his parents to send for Martin, which they did immediately. They fed the stranger, who was eager to be on his way, and then fixed breakfast for the family and Martin, who usually came quickly when called. The food was on the table by 8:00 a.m., but Martin did not arrive as expected. They waited and waited until finally, at 12:30, they "saw him walking with a slow and measured tread towards the house," looking down the whole time.[13]

Martin sat on the fence for a while before coming in to sit at the table. "He took up his knife and fork as if he were going to use them," Joseph's mother said, "but immediately dropped them." Joseph's brother Hyrum asked Martin if he was sick, and Martin began pressing his hands to his temples, crying, "Oh, I have lost my soul! I have lost my soul!"

Joseph Smith's parents' farmhouse, Manchester, New York, where he questioned Martin Harris.

Martin Harris, first scribe for the Book of Mormon translation.

Joseph, who had tried to look calm, now exclaimed, "Martin, have you lost that manuscript? Have you broken your oath, and brought down condemnation upon my head, as well as your own?"

"Yes, it is gone," Martin confessed, "and I know not where."[14]

Joseph could hardly be consoled, worrying that the stressful news might kill the weakened Emma when he told her. "And how shall I appear before the Lord?" he asked. "Of what rebuke am I not worthy from the angel of the Most High?"

Joseph wept, grieved, and paced the floor until nearly sundown before finally eating something. The next day, he started for home. "We parted with heavy hearts," his mother wrote, "for it now appeared that all which we had so fondly anticipated, and which had been the source of so much secret gratification, had in a moment fled, and fled for ever."[15]

Martin had broken his promise, and the 116 manuscript pages had disappeared. He "suffered temporally as well as spiritually" for the loss. Some of his crops failed, and he experienced deep anguish.[16]

"I also was chastened," Joseph wrote, and the plates were "taken from me ... for a season." Joseph returned to Harmony, and after a time of sore repentance, he received the plates again. But he still needed someone to write as he dictated the translation. He asked the Lord "to send him a scribe."[17]

Three days later, on April 5, 1829, Oliver Cowdery arrived in Harmony, brought by spiritual impressions and Joseph's brother Samuel. Oliver had been teaching school and boarding with Joseph's parents when he learned about the golden plates. He was the full-time scribe Joseph needed.[18]

On Monday, April 6, Joseph and Emma closed on the home where they'd been living, which they bought from Emma's brother. On Tuesday, Joseph and

Oliver began translating the plates in earnest. From that point on, Oliver served as principal scribe for the translation, though others stepped in from time to time.[19]

The pace of translation was stunning: about eight pages a day—remarkable even for skilled translators.[20] "Day after day I continued, uninterrupted, to write from his mouth, as he translated," Oliver Cowdery wrote.[21] They probably began with the portion of Mosiah that Joseph still had and continued to the end of Moroni, then moved to the small plates of Nephi, finishing at Words of Mormon.[22] The translation of the small plates covered the same time period as the lost 116 pages, but from a spiritual rather than a historical perspective.[23] By the end of June, the translation was complete.[24]

In early June, Oliver's friend David Whitmer came down to Harmony from Fayette, New York, with a two-horse wagon. He took Joseph and Oliver back to the home of David's parents, Peter and Mary Whitmer, so the men could finish the translation without worries about supporting themselves or the increasing persecution where they had been living. Emma soon joined them.[25]

Mary Whitmer felt burdened by the extra persons staying with her family. When she went out to milk cows one evening, she ran into a man who explained the important work being done in her home. He untied a knapsack and showed her the golden plates before vanishing. Thereafter, Mary's household duties seemed easier.[26] Soon five of her sons and six other people would also see the ancient book.

As Joseph translated the record and received additional revelation, he learned God would grant special witnesses—three in particular—the privilege to see and testify about the plates. Oliver Cowdery, David Whitmer, and Martin

Page from the original Book of Mormon manuscript beginning in the handwriting of Oliver Cowdery. At the point shown by the arrow, an unidentified scribe begins writing the famous verse that is now 1 Nephi 3:7. Note the continuous flow of the dictation with little punctuation.

Harris asked if they could be the three. Joseph prayed and received direction that they should indeed be the ones.[27]

Later, near the Whitmer home, Oliver, David, and Martin were shown the plates, the interpreters, and other sacred objects. They testified "that an Angel of God came down from heaven, and he brought and laid before our eyes, that we beheld and saw the plates, and the engravings thereon." They also heard God's voice declare "that they [had] been translated by the gift and power of God."[28]

Not long thereafter, this time in the woods near his parents' home, Joseph showed the plates to his father, his brothers Hyrum and Samuel, David Whitmer's four brothers, and their brother-in-law Hiram Page. The eight men testified that "we have seen and hefted, and know of a surety, that the said Smith has got the plates of which we have spoken."[29]

"After these witnesses returned to the house," Joseph's mother said, "the angel again made his appearance . . . at which time Joseph delivered up the plates into the angel's hands." He had fulfilled the charge he received and could breathe a sigh of relief that the plates were safely out of his hands and that others could bear witness that they really existed.[30]

Future generations tried mightily to explain how a largely untutored youth could dictate a complex record of nearly five hundred manuscript pages in a single draft over fewer than ninety working days. Millions have accepted Joseph's explanation as the only plausible one: that he did it "by the gift and power of God."

PREFACE.

To the Reader—

As many false reports have been circulated respecting the following work, and also many unlawful measures taken by evil designing persons to destroy me, and also the work, I would inform you that I translated, by the gift and power of God, and caused to be written, one hundred and sixteen pages, the which I took from the Book of Lehi, which was an account abridged from the plates of Lehi, by the hand of Mormon; which said account, some person or persons have stolen and kept from me, notwithstanding my utmost exertions to recover it again—and being commanded of the Lord that I should not translate the same over again, for Satan had put it into their hearts to tempt the Lord their God, by altering the words, that they did read contrary from that which I translated and caused to be written; and if I should bring forth the same words again, or, in other words, if I should translate the same over again, they would publish that which they had stolen, and Satan would stir up the hearts of this generation, that they might not receive this work: but behold, the Lord said unto me, I will not suffer that Satan shall accomplish his evil design in this thing: therefore thou shalt translate from the plates of Nephi, until ye come to that which ye have translated, which ye have retained; and

Opening page of Joseph Smith's preface to the first edition of the Book of Mormon, explaining the loss of the 116 manuscript pages.

behold ye shall publish it as the record of Nephi; and thus I will confound those who have altered my words. I will not suffer that they shall destroy my work; yea, I will shew unto them that my wisdom is greater than the cunning of the Devil. Wherefore, to be obedient unto the commandments of God, I have, through his grace and mercy, accomplished that which he hath commanded me respecting this thing. I would also inform you that the plates of which hath been spoken, were found in the township of Manchester, Ontario county, New-York.

THE AUTHOR.

Second page of Joseph Smith's preface to the first edition.
This preface was Joseph's first published history.

The building in Palmyra, New York, that housed Egbert B. Grandin's print shop, where the first edition of the Book of Mormon was printed.

Chapter Three
THE FIRST EDITION, 1830

Joseph's thoughts turned to publishing the Book of Mormon even before he finished the translation. On June 11, 1829, he took a break from translating and visited the federal court for the Northern District of New York. There he applied for a copyright to the Book of Mormon, depositing a printed copy of a title page he had brought with him.

Federal law granted copyrights to "authors and proprietors," and the term "authors" included translators. The court clerk dutifully filled out a copyright certificate, copying information onto it from the title page of the Book of Mormon. He entered a copy of the certificate in a bound register for future reference before giving the document to Joseph.[1]

Around the same time, Joseph began looking for a publisher, which proved challenging. He went to Egbert B. Grandin, a young printer in Palmyra, New York, near where Joseph's parents lived. Together, Grandin and his friend Luther Howard ran a three-story book business on Main Street. Grandin printed pages on the third story and lowered them down to Howard, who bound them in his second-story shop. They then sold the books in the first-story bookstore.[2]

Original copyright registration of the Book of Mormon, June 11, 1829.

THE FIRST EDITION, 1830

Printing the Book of Mormon in Palmyra was Joseph's first choice. He planned to go back to Harmony to live with Emma in their new home, leaving Oliver, Martin, and Hyrum to oversee the printing. Oliver could stay with the Smiths, who lived south of Palmyra village on Stafford Road, saving costs. But the strong attitudes that drove Joseph from Palmyra in the first place led Grandin to turn down the first invitation to print the book.[3]

Joseph and Martin next went to Rochester, which was more than twenty miles away. Rochester was a fast-growing city up the Erie Canal from Palmyra where they hoped to find someone open-minded and ambitious enough to take on the project. After being turned down twice more, they finally found a Rochester publisher willing to print the book. Before signing a contract with him, however, the men decided to return to Grandin and try one more time.

Grandin had two concerns. First, he doubted the book would sell well enough to cover his costs and turn a profit. The project was big for a young country printer, and he wasn't eager to tie up his equipment on a losing proposition. Second, not all of his neighbors were enthusiastic about the book, and he didn't want to disappoint them or make them think he bought into this newfangled faith in any way.

Egbert B. Grandin.

Martin Harris solved the first problem by agreeing to mortgage his farm to assure Grandin that he would be paid. And passing up the offer wouldn't stop the book from being printed, Joseph and Martin pointed out, since a Rochester publisher was willing to print it. Not wanting to lose a sure profit, Grandin counseled with friends, who agreed with his printing the book as long as he did it strictly for business reasons. Grandin told Joseph he would do it.[4]

The contract called for Grandin to print five thousand copies for three thousand dollars, a large print order for its day. Grandin went to work advertising for more help in his print shop and ordering a new type font—he would need a lot of metal type for this job.[5]

Joseph, meanwhile, made preparations. First, he asked Oliver to make a copy of the whole manuscript of the Book of Mormon. After losing the 116 pages, Joseph didn't want to risk losing pages again. Second, he charged Oliver to take only one copy of the manuscript to the printer at a time "so that if one copy should get destroyed, there would still be a copy remaining." Third, he said "that in going to and from the office, he [Oliver] should always have a guard to attend him" to protect the manuscript. Finally, he directed that a guard keep watch over the house "both night and day" to keep "malicious persons" from coming in to destroy the manuscript. "After giving these instructions," his mother remembered, "Joseph returned to Pennsylvania."[6]

It took Oliver, Hyrum, and another scribe more time to copy the manuscript than it took Joseph to dictate it originally. That was partly because Oliver and Hyrum also had other duties to perform. They worked hard to stay ahead of the printer, but at one point, the printing may have gotten ahead of the copying, and the original manuscript, instead of the copy, was used to set type for the printed book.[7]

The printing job was reportedly the largest ever done in the county, and both Grandin (the printer) and Howard (the binder) had to take on extra help to do the job.[8]

Grandin invited an experienced printer named John H. Gilbert to set type for the Book of Mormon. According to Gilbert, when Grandin was ready to start the printing, he notified Martin Harris, who lived nearby. Martin got word to the Smith family, and Hyrum carried the first twenty-four pages of the manuscript to the print shop. Gilbert remembered that when Hyrum walked into the shop, he had part of the manuscript "under his vest," with his "vest and coat closely buttoned over it." That night, Hyrum retrieved the pages and took them home, repeating the routine "with the same watchfulness" the next morning.⁹

John H. Gilbert, who set the type for the first edition of the Book of Mormon.

The manuscript remained safe, just as Joseph had hoped, but soon another problem arose. The printers set the type to create large sheets of sixteen pages each that would later be folded, bound, and trimmed to form books. After printing five thousand copies of the first sheet, they set them aside and set type for the second sixteen-page sheet. It took from August 1829 to March 1830 to print the nearly three million pages needed for the first edition of the Book of Mormon.¹⁰

Grandin allowed his friend Abner Cole to use his print shop at nights and on Sundays when Grandin's own employees rested. Cole published a small-format newspaper called *The Reflector* that he used to poke fun at others under his pen name, Obadiah Dogberry. As Cole was working in the print shop, he noticed the uncut sheets of the Book of Mormon waiting for binding and decided to pirate the book in his paper. In his last issue of the paper for December 1829, he published a teaser, "'Gold Bible' next week," which let his readers know of his plan.

Oliver and Hyrum confronted Cole about his wrongdoing one Sunday morning at the print shop. "Mr. Cole," Hyrum said, "what right have you to print the Book of Mormon in this manner? Do you not know that we have secured the copyright?"

"It is none of your business," Cole replied. "I have hired the press, and will print what I please."

The more Hyrum tried to dissuade him, the angrier Cole became. Hyrum finally went home and consulted with his father, who said Joseph needed to know about the problem. Father Smith left for Harmony and returned with Joseph the next Sunday.

Going to the print shop, Joseph approached Cole about his piracy. Cole took off his coat and went at Joseph, pounding his fists together and yelling: "Do you want to fight, sir? Do you want to fight? I will publish just what I please. Now, if you want to fight, just come on."

Joseph calmly assured the agitated man he did not want to fight and then added quietly, "Mr. Cole, there is law, and you will find that out, if you do not understand it."

BY O. DOGBERRY, Esq.]

[From the Book of Mormon.]

THE FIRST BOOK OF NEPHI.

HIS REIGN AND MINISTRY.

CHAPTER I.

I, Nephi, having been born of goodly parents, therefore I was taught somewhat in all the learning of my father; and having seen many afflictions in the course of my days—nevertheless, having been highly favored of the Lord in all my days; yea, having had a great knowledge of the goodness and the mysteries of God, thererefore I make a record of my proceedings in my days; yea, I make a record in the language of my father, which consists of the learning of the Jews and the language of the Egyptians. And I know that the record which I make, to be true; and I make it with mine own hand; and I make it according to my knowledge.

For it came to pass, in the commencement of the first year of the reign of Zedekiah, king of Judah, (my father Lehi having dwelt at Jerusalem in all his days;) and in that same year there came many prophets, prophesying unto the people, that they must repent, or the great city Jerusalem must be destroyed. Wherefore it came to pass, that my father Lehi, as he went forth, prayed unto the Lord, yea, even with all his heart, in behalf of his people.

In the January 2, 1830, issue of The Reflector, *Abner Cole began pirating the Book of Mormon.*

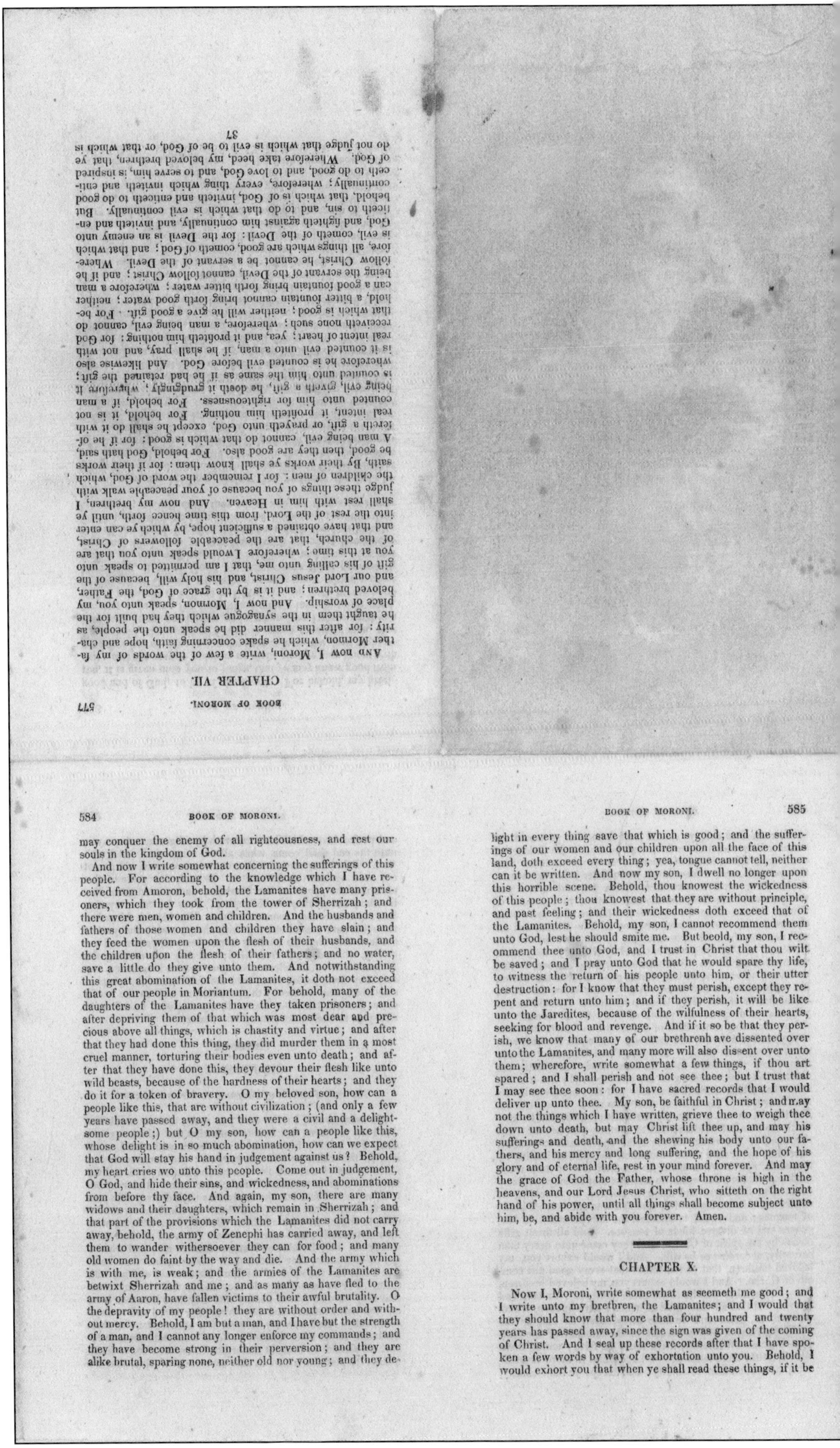

CHAPTER VII.

AND now I, Moroni, write a few of the words of my father Mormon, which he spake concerning faith, hope and charity: for after this manner did he speak unto the people, as he taught them in the synagogue which they had built for the place of worship. And now I, Mormon, speak unto you, my beloved brethren; and it is by the grace of God, the Father, and our Lord Jesus Christ, and his holy will, because of the gift of his calling unto me, that I am permitted to speak unto you at this time; wherefore I would speak unto you that are of the church, that are the peaceable followers of Christ, and that have obtained a sufficient hope, by which ye can enter into the rest of the Lord, from this time hence forth, until ye shall rest with him in Heaven. And now my brethren, I judge these things of you because of your peaceable walk with the children of men: for I remember the word of God, which saith, By their works ye shall know them: for if their works be good, then they are good also. For behold, God hath said, A man being evil, cannot do that which is good: for if he offereth a gift, or prayeth unto God, except he shall do it with real intent, it profiteth him nothing. For behold, it is not counted unto him for righteousness. For behold, if a man being evil, giveth a gift, he doeth it grudgingly; wherefore it is counted unto him the same as if he had retained the gift; wherefore he is counted evil before God. And likewise also is it counted evil unto a man, if he shall pray, and not with real intent of heart; yea, and it profiteth him nothing: for God receiveth none such; wherefore, a man being evil, cannot do that which is good; neither will he give a good gift. For behold, a bitter fountain cannot bring forth good water; neither can a good fountain bring forth bitter water; wherefore a man being the servant of the Devil, cannot follow Christ; and if he follow Christ, he cannot be a servant of the Devil. Wherefore, all things which are good, cometh of God; and that which is evil, cometh of the Devil: for the Devil is an enemy unto God, and fighteth against him continually, and inviteth and enticeth to sin, and to do that which is evil continually. But behold, that which is of God, inviteth and enticeth to do good continually; wherefore, every thing which inviteth and enticeth to do good, and to love God, and to serve him, is inspired of God. Wherefore take heed, my beloved brethren, that ye do not judge that which is evil to be of God, or that which is

may conquer the enemy of all righteousness, and rest our souls in the kingdom of God.

And now I write somewhat concerning the sufferings of this people. For according to the knowledge which I have received from Amoron, behold, the Lamanites have many prisoners, which they took from the tower of Sherrizah; and there were men, women and children. And the husbands and fathers of those women and children they have slain; and they feed the women upon the flesh of their husbands, and the children upon the flesh of their fathers; and no water, save a little do they give unto them. And notwithstanding this great abomination of the Lamanites, it doth not exceed that of our people in Moriantum. For behold, many of the daughters of the Lamanites have they taken prisoners; and after depriving them of that which was most dear and precious above all things, which is chastity and virtue; and after that they had done this thing, they did murder them in a most cruel manner, torturing their bodies even unto death; and after that they have done this, they devour their flesh like unto wild beasts, because of the hardness of their hearts; and they do it for a token of bravery. O my beloved son, how can a people like this, that are without civilization; (and only a few years have passed away, and they were a civil and a delightsome people;) but O my son, how can a people like this, whose delight is in so much abomination, how can we expect that God will stay his hand in judgement against us? Behold, my heart cries wo unto this people. Come out in judgement, O God, and hide their sins, and wickedness, and abominations from before thy face. And again, my son, there are many widows and their daughters, which remain in Sherrizah; and that part of the provisions which the Lamanites did not carry away, behold, the army of Zenephi has carried away, and left them to wander withersoever they can for food; and many old women do faint by the way and die. And the army which is with me, is weak; and the armies of the Lamanites are betwixt Sherrizah and me; and as many as have fled to the army of Aaron, have fallen victims to their awful brutality. O the depravity of my people! they are without order and without mercy. Behold, I am but a man, and I have but the strength of a man, and I cannot any longer enforce my commands; and they have become strong in their perversion; and they are alike brutal, sparing none, neither old nor young; and they de-

light in every thing save that which is good; and the sufferings of our women and our children upon all the face of this land, doth exceed every thing; yea, tongue cannot tell, neither can it be written. And now my son, I dwell no longer upon this horrible scene. Behold, thou knowest the wickedness of this people; thou knowest that they are without principle, and past feeling; and their wickedness doth exceed that of the Lamanites. Behold, my son, I cannot recommend them unto God, lest he should smite me. But beold, my son, I recommend thee unto God, and I trust in Christ that thou wilt be saved; and I pray unto God that he would spare thy life, to witness the return of his people unto him, or their utter destruction: for I know that they must perish, except they repent and return unto him; and if they perish, it will be like unto the Jaredites, because of the wilfulness of their hearts, seeking for blood and revenge. And if it so be that they perish, we know that many of our brethrenh ave dissented over unto the Lamanites, and many more will also dissent over unto them; wherefore, write somewhat a few things, if thou art spared; and I shall perish and not see thee; but I trust that I may see thee soon: for I have sacred records that I would deliver up unto thee. My son, be faithful in Christ; and may not the things which I have written, grieve thee to weigh thee down unto death, but may Christ lift thee up, and may his sufferings and death, and the shewing his body unto our fathers, and his mercy and long suffering, and the hope of his glory and of eternal life, rest in your mind forever. And may the grace of God the Father, whose throne is high in the heavens, and our Lord Jesus Christ, who sitteth on the right hand of his power, until all things shall become subject unto him, be, and abide with you forever. Amen.

CHAPTER X.

Now I, Moroni, write somewhat as seemeth me good; and I write unto my brethren, the Lamanites; and I would that they should know that more than four hundred and twenty years has passed away, since the sign was given of the coming of Christ. And I seal up these records after that I have spoken a few words by way of exhortation unto you. Behold, I would exhort you that when ye shall read these things, if it be

An original uncut sheet of the Book of Mormon.

BOOK OF MORONI. 580

be unto the children of men, for it is because of unbelief, and all is vain: for no man can be saved, according to the words of Christ, save they shall have faith in his name; wherefore, if these things have ceased, then has faith ceased also; and awful is the state of man: for they are as though there had been no redemption made. But behold, my beloved brethren, I judge better things of you, for I judge that ye have faith in Christ, because of your meekness: for if ye have not faith in him, then ye are not fit to be numbered among the people of his church. And again my beloved brethren, I would speak unto you concerning hope. How is it that ye can attain unto faith, save ye shall have hope? And what is it that ye shall hope for? Behold I say unto you, That ye shall have hope through the atonement of Christ and the power of his resurrection, to be raised unto life eternal; and this because of your faith in him according to the promise: wherefore, if a man have faith, he must needs have hope: for without faith there cannot be any hope. And again: Behold I say unto you, That lowly of heart: if so, his faith and hope is vain, for none is acceptable before God, save the meek and lowly of heart; and if a man be meek and lowly in heart, and confesses by the power of the Holy Ghost, that Jesus is the Christ, he must needs have charity: for if he have not charity, he is nothing; wherefore he must needs have charity. And charity suffereth long, and is kind, and envieth not, and is not puffed up, seeketh not her own, is not easily provoked, thinketh no evil, and rejoiceth not in iniquity, but rejoiceth in the truth, beareth all things, believeth all things, hopeth all things, endureth all things; wherefore, my beloved brethren, if ye have not charity, ye are nothing, for charity never faileth. Wherefore, cleave unto charity, which is the greatest of all, for all things must fail; but charity is the pure love of Christ, and it endureth forever; and whoso is found possessed of it, at the last day it shall be well with them. Wherefore, my beloved brethren, pray unto the Father with all the energy of heart, that ye may be filled with this love which he hath bestowed upon all who are true followers of his Son Jesus Christ, that ye may become the sons of God, that when he shall appear, we shall be like him: for we shall see him as he is, that we may have this hope, that we may be purified even as he is pure. Amen.

BOOK OF MORONI. 581

CHAPTER VIII.

An epistle of my father Mormon, written to me, Moroni; and it was written unto me soon after my calling to the ministry. And on this wise did he write unto me, saying: My beloved son Moroni, I rejoice exceedingly that your Lord Jesus Christ hath been mindful of you, and hath called you to his ministry, and to his holy work. I am mindful of you always in my prayers, continually praying unto God the Father, in the name of his holy child, Jesus, that he, through his infinite goodness and grace, will keep you through the endurance of faith on his name to the end.

And now my son, I speak unto you concerning that which grieveth me exceedingly: for it grieveth me that there should disputations rise among you. For if I have learned the truth, there has been disputations among you concerning the baptism of your little children. And now my son, I desire that ye should labor diligently, that this gross error should be removed from among you: for, for this intent I have written this epistle. For immediately after I had learned these things of you, I inquired of the Lord concerning the matter. And the word of the Lord came to me by the power of the Holy Ghost, saying, Listen to the words of Christ, your Redeemer, your Lord and your God. Behold, I came into the world not to call the righteous, but sinners to repentance; the whole need no physician, but they that are sick; wherefore little children are whole, for they are not capable of committing sin; wherefore the curse of Adam is taken from them in me, that it hath no power over them: and the law of circumcision is done away in me. And after this manner did the Holy Ghost manifest the word of God unto me; wherefore my beloved son, I know that it is solemn mockery before God, that ye should baptize little children. Behold I say unto you, that this thing shall ye teach, repentance and baptism unto they which are accountable and capable of committing sin; yea, teach parents that they must repent and be baptized, and humble themselves as their little children, and they shall all be saved with their little children; and their little children need no repentance, neither baptism. Behold, baptism is unto repentance to the fulfilling the commandments unto the remission of sins. But little children are alive in Christ, even from the foundation of the world: if not so, God is a partial God, and also a changeble God, and a respecter to persons: for how many little children

588 BOOK OF MORONI.

unto the remission of your sins, that ye become holy without spot. And now I bid unto all, farewell. I soon go to rest in the paradise of God, until my spirit and body shall again reunite, and I am brought forth triumphant through the air, to meet you before the pleasing bar of the great Jehovah, the Eternal Judge of both quick and dead. Amen.

THE END.

THE TESTIMONY OF THREE WITNESSES.

Be it known unto all nations, kindreds, tongues, and people, unto whom this work shall come, that we, through the grace of God the Father, and our Lord Jesus Christ, have seen the plates which contain this record, which is a record of the people of Nephi, and also of the Lamanites, his brethren, and also of the people of Jared, which came from the tower, of which hath been spoken; and we also know that they have been translated by the gift and power of God, for his voice hath declared it unto us; wherefore we know of a surety, that the work is true. And we also testify that we have seen the engravings which are upon the plates: and they have been shewn unto us by the power of God, and not of man. And we declare with words of soberness, that an angel of God came down from heaven, and he brought and laid before our eyes, that we beheld and saw the plates, and the engravings thereon; and we know that it is by the grace of God the Father, and our Lord Jesus Christ, that we beheld and bear record that these things are true; and it is marvellous in our eyes: Nevertheless, the voice of the Lord commanded us that we should bear record of it; wherefore, to be obedient unto the commandments of God, we bear testimony of these things.—And we know that if we are faithful in Christ, we shall rid our garments of the blood of all men, and be found spotless before the judgement seat of Christ, and shall dwell with him eternally in the heavens. And the honor be to the Father, and to the Son, and to the Holy Ghost, which is one God. Amen.

OLIVER COWDERY,
DAVID WHITMER,
MARTIN HARRIS.

At that, Cole cooled down and finally agreed to submit the matter to arbitration. He was ultimately ordered to stop his unethical activity and did so.[11] Cole's piracy, however, cost him at least one subscription. On March 11, Luther Howard, the binder for the Book of Mormon, wrote to Cole, "When the present series of the *Reflector* is completed, you will please to erase my name from your list of subscribers."[12]

Finally, on March 26, 1830, a notice appeared in Grandin's own newspaper, the *Wayne Sentinel*. It reproduced the information from the title page of the Book of Mormon and announced, "The above work, containing about 600 pages, large Duodecimo, is now for sale, wholesale and retail, at the Palmyra Bookstore, by HOWARD & GRANDIN."[13] At last, the book was available to the public in an authorized form.

Despite the book's notoriety, people in the Palmyra area resolved to boycott its sale. The volume sold for $1.75 a copy, but few people bought it, and the price soon dropped to $1.25. Martin Harris tried selling copies and was grieved when they wouldn't sell. He asked Joseph Smith for a revelation on the subject, and Joseph received one commanding Martin, "Thou shalt not covet thine own property, but impart it freely to the printing of the Book of Mormon."[14]

A year after the book was released, it still hadn't sold enough copies to cover the printing costs, and Martin fulfilled the commandment he had received. On April 7, 1831, he sold 150¼ acres of his farm for $3,000 to Thomas Lakey, who agreed to pay him over the next year and a half. On January 28, 1832, Lakey sold the property for $3,300 in gold, keeping $300 and giving Martin the $3,000 he needed to meet his obligation to Grandin.[15]

Martin's sacrifice had made it possible to publish the Book of Mormon to the world.

THE

BOOK OF MORMON:

AN ACCOUNT WRITTEN BY THE HAND OF MOR- MON, UPON PLATES TAKEN FROM THE PLATES OF NEPHI.

Wherefore it is an abridgment of the Record of the People of Nephi; and also of the Lamanites; written to the Lamanites, which are a remnant of the House of Israel; and also to Jew and Gentile; written by way of commandment, and also by the spirit of Prophesy and of Revelation. Written, and sealed up, and hid up unto the LORD, that they might not be destroyed; to come forth by the gift and power of GOD unto the interpretation thereof; sealed by the hand of Moroni, and hid up unto the LORD, to come forth in due time by the way of Gentile; the interpretation thereof by the gift of GOD; an abridgment taken from the Book of Ether.

Also, which is a Record of the People of Jared, which were scattered at the time the LORD confounded the language of the people when they were building a tower to get to Heaven: which is to shew unto the remnant of the House of Israel how great things the LORD hath done for their fathers; and that they may know the covenants of the LORD, that they are not cast off forever; and also to the convincing of the Jew and Gentile that JESUS is the CHRIST, the ETERNAL GOD, manifesting Himself unto all nations. And now if there be fault, it be the mistake of men; wherefore condemn not the things of GOD, that ye may be found spotless at the judgment seat of CHRIST.

BY JOSEPH SMITH, JUNIOR,
AUTHOR AND PROPRIETOR.

PALMYRA:
PRINTED BY E. B. GRANDIN, FOR THE AUTHOR.
1830.

Title page of the first edition of the Book of Mormon.

Kirtland Temple, 1907. The second edition of the Book of Mormon was printed behind the temple in a shop that burned down in 1837. (Chair with arm desk in foreground was owned by Joseph Smith.)

Chapter Four
THE SECOND EDITION, 1837

Eleven days after Grandin and Howard announced the Book of Mormon was available, believers in the gospel it contained met at the home of Peter and Mary Whitmer in Fayette, New York. There they legally organized the Church of Christ, renamed eight years later The Church of Jesus Christ of Latter-day Saints.[1]

As the Church grew and its missionaries traveled across the United States and into Canada, the first edition of five thousand copies of the Book of Mormon gradually ran out, and plans were formed to publish a second edition.

In the summer of 1831, Joseph Smith traveled to Independence, Missouri. There he received a revelation identifying the area as "the land of promise" (which was a Book of Mormon term) "and the place for the city of Zion." The revelation also directed William W. Phelps, a recently converted newspaperman, to go to Zion "and be established as a printer unto the church."[2]

In June 1832, Phelps began printing the Church's first newspaper, *The Evening and the Morning Star,* in Independence. From the very first issue, he used the paper to publish Joseph Smith's revelations so Church members could have access to them.[3] A year after starting the paper, Phelps also began publishing the Book of Mormon in the *Star*. He knew the paper was read not just by Church members but also by neighbors in the frontier town who viewed the fast-growing Mormon population with suspicion.[4]

Explaining that Church members viewed the Book of Mormon "as a heavenly treasure," Phelps acknowledged that "few, very few of our fellow men . . . know any thing about the merits of this sacred volume." He announced that part of the book would appear in each issue of the *Star* "until it is finished." This would give people a chance "to read for themselves" so they could understand why the Saints were gathering in the area.[5]

Meanwhile, Phelps was also negotiating with Joseph Smith and other Church leaders living in Kirtland, Ohio—the Church's temporary headquarters—to print a whole new edition of the Book of Mormon in Missouri. They wrote back in June 1833, right after Phelps began publishing excerpts in the *Star*. "As soon as we can get time," they explained, "we will review the manuscripts of the Book of Mormon, after which they will be forwarded to you."[6]

In the July issue of the *Star*, Phelps announced a change in plans. "In our last number," he noted, "we commenced the publication of the Book of Mormon, but having altered our calculation, it is stopped." Why? "Our reason is, that, at no very distant period, we shall print the Book of Mormon and the Testament, and bind them in one volume: therefore to continue it in the *Star* would be superfluous."[7]

Not long after this announcement appeared, however, vigilantes marched to the print shop in Independence. Upset by another article in the paper, they evicted Phelps's family from the first story of the building and tore the two-story structure to the ground. The attack stalled the Church's printing projects,

THE BOOK OF MORMON.

Notwithstanding the church of Christ has received the fulness of the gospel from the book of Mormon, and every member as a true disciple of the blessed Savior, studies it as a heavenly treasure, yet few, very few of our fellow men in the world, know any thing about the merits of this sacred volume. We therefore, have concluded to commence its publication in the Star, and shall continue from number to number until it is finished.

By this means the world will have an opportunity to read for themselves, and prepare for the great days to come. By this means those who are seeking for truth can find it, and compare the book of Mormon with the bible, and witness the great doings of the Lord in these last days, in bringing forth his everlasting covenant for the gathering of his elect, and the restoration of the tribes, and scattered remnants of Israel from the four quarters of the earth.

We have again inserted the articles and covenants according to our promise in a previous number, for the benefit of our brethren abroad who have not the first number of the first volume. As there were, some errors which had got into them by transcribing, we have since obtained the original copy and made the necessary corrections.

CHAPTER I.

I, NEPHI, having been born of goodly parents, therefore I was taught somewhat in all the learning of my father; and having seen many afflictions in the course of my days—nevertheless, having been highly favored of the Lord in all my days; yea, having had a great knowledge of the goodness and the mysteries of God, therefore I make a record of my proceedings in my days; yea, I make a record in the language of my father, which consists of the learning of the Jews and the language of the Egyptians. And I know that the record which I make, to be true; and I make it with mine own hand; and I make it according to my knowledge.

The Evening and the Morning Star *began printing the Book of Mormon in its pages in 1833.*

W. W. Phelps, designated by scripture as the Church printer.

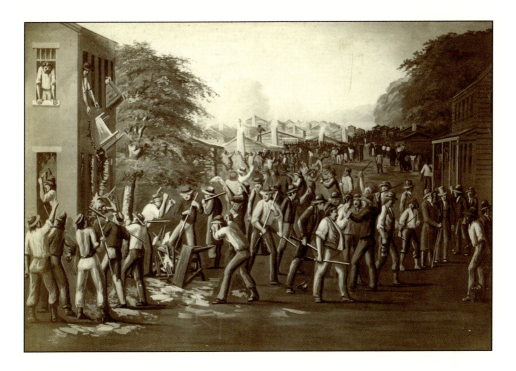

Vigilantes destroy the Church print shop in Independence, Missouri.

including Phelps's plans to print the Book of Mormon and New Testament together.[8]

The main printing operations of the Church then shifted to Kirtland, Ohio, where eventually a print shop was built west of the hill on which a new temple was being constructed. Parley P. Pratt, an apostle of the Church, and John Goodson, a convert from Canada, obtained permission from Joseph Smith to have a second edition of the Book of Mormon printed in this shop in the winter of 1836–37 by Oliver Cowdery and Co.[9]

Joseph let Oliver use the printer's manuscript of the Book of Mormon for this edition, but not before Joseph reviewed it, as he earlier told Phelps he planned to do. "Joseph Smith went through the printer's manuscript and altered the grammar of the text to reflect standard English rather than Joseph's native upstate New York English," concluded one linguist who studied the changes.[10]

Upheld by the Church as a translator, Joseph refined the language of the first edition, which may have suited early converts in New York, to make it more universally acceptable in the English-speaking world.[11] This was fortunate because the second edition would be used to introduce the Church in the British Isles and beyond. Parley P. Pratt and John Goodson, publishers of the book, would be among the early Latter-day Saint missionaries to travel overseas.[12]

Pratt and Goodson knew copies of the book would travel farther than they could in their lives. In their preface to the second edition, they anticipated that "this book will be conveyed to places which circumstances will render it impossible for us to visit, and be perused by thousands whose faces we may never see on this side of eternity."[13]

Earlier, in Missouri, Phelps had planned to bind the second edition of the Book of Mormon with the New Testament, giving the Church its first combination scriptures. Pratt and Goodson also decided to print two books in one volume. But their plan was to combine the second edition of the Book of Mormon with the Doctrine and Covenants, a book of latter-day scripture printed in 1835 that was, like the Book of Mormon, then in short supply.[14]

They also decided to shrink the size of the volume for two related reasons. First, they wanted the book to be "a pocket companion." The first edition of the Book of Mormon had been sized for the bookshelf, and they wanted the second edition to be small enough for people to carry around and read easily.[15]

Second, they knew missionaries would carry copies with them in their travels, often on foot. Printing the book "in a condensed form," they decided, offered "greater convenience to elders, and others, who convey the same to different parts."[16]

Printer's manuscript of Mosiah 28:12–29:4, showing Joseph Smith's corrections in heavy black ink for the second edition of the Book of Mormon.

Willard Richards.

Pratt and Goodson announced their intention in the preface to their edition of the Book of Mormon, which was on the first set of pages run off by the printer. By the time the last part of the Book of Mormon was almost finished, however, the publishers realized their plan would not work. Near the end of the book, they added a note "To the Reader."

"Contrary to our expectations, when the foregoing work was commenced," they wrote, "we have been induced to abandon the idea of attaching to it the Book of Doctrine and Covenants. We came to this conclusion from the fact, that the two connected, would make a volume, entirely too unwieldy for the purpose intended, that of a pocket companion."[17]

They did succeed, however, in making an edition of the Book of Mormon that was convenient to carry. The second edition was decidedly smaller than the first. John Goodson in particular must have appreciated the difference when he left for England on a mission in June 1837, taking as many as two hundred copies of the book with him.[18]

For a variety of reasons, the Church in Kirtland faced widespread dissent in 1837. The missionary force that went to England that year with the second edition of the Book of Mormon helped to strengthen the Church by laying the foundation for fresh waves of British converts in the years to come.[19]

In the short run, however, the difficulties in Kirtland led to the loss of the printing operation. They also led Joseph Smith to flee Kirtland for Missouri. After he left, the print shop caught fire.[20]

Willard Richards was among the missionaries who went to England with the second edition. His sister Hepzibah wrote him, saying the shop was sold at auction to "one of the dissenters." At one o'clock the next morning, she said, "Cousin Mary waked me, and said that Kirtland was all in flames. It proved to be the printing office—the fire was then in its height and in one hour it was consumed with all its contents. The temple and other buildings [were] badly scorched."[21]

Another Kirtland resident who soon followed Joseph Smith west but was still in Ohio at the time wrote that "the office was consumed with fire . . . together with all its contents," including "many Books of Mormon belonging to the Brethren."[22]

Pratt and Goodson originally intended to print five thousand copies of the second edition, the same number as was printed in the first edition.[23] In the end, they may have printed only three thousand, perhaps because of the poverty and dissent in Kirtland. The fire reduced the number of surviving copies further.

The 1837 Kirtland edition of the Book of Mormon thus became scarcer than the first edition.[24] Another factor that perhaps contributed to the eventual scarcity was that it was a pocket edition, meant to be carried around and read—and eventually worn out by use.

Yet the impact of the book would remain, a testimony to the sacrifice of those whose work led to its publication. And the testimony of its publishers, included in their preface to the second edition, would travel across time and space to reach many thousands.

As they thought about the people who would read their edition in distant lands, Parley P. Pratt and John Goodson wrote of the Book of Mormon, "We cannot consistently let the opportunity pass, without expressing our sincere conviction of its truth, and the great and glorious purposes it must effect, in the restoration of the house of Israel, and the ushering in of that blessed day when the knowledge of God will cover the earth, and one universal peace pervade all people."[25]

When the print shop behind the Kirtland Temple caught fire in 1837, the flames could be seen for miles. The fire destroyed many copies of the second edition of the Book of Mormon.

THE
BOOK OF MORMON:

AN ACCOUNT WRITTEN BY THE HAND OF MOR-
MON, UPON PLATES TAKEN FROM
THE PLATES OF NEPHI.

Wherefore it is an abridgment of the record of the people of Nephi, and also of the Lamanites; written to the Lamanites, who are a remnant of the house of Israel; and also to Jew and Gentile: written by way of commandment, and also by the spirit of prophecy and of revelation. Written, and sealed up, and hid up unto the LORD, that they might not be destroyed; to come forth by the gift and power of GOD unto the interpretation thereof: sealed by the hand of Moroni, and hid up unto the LORD, to come forth in due time by the way of Gentile; the interpretation thereof by the gift of GOD:

An abridgment taken from the book of Ether: also, which is a record of the people of Jared; who were scattered at the time the LORD confounded the language of the people when they were building a tower to get to heaven: which is to shew unto the remnant of the house of Israel what great things the LORD hath done for their fathers; and that they may know the covenants of the LORD, that they are not cast off forever; and also to the convincing of the Jew and Gentile that JESUS is the CHRIST, the ETERNAL GOD, manifesting himself unto all nations. And now if there are faults, they are the mistakes of men; wherefore condemn not the things of GOD, that ye may be found spotless at the judgment seat of CHRIST.

TRANSLATED BY
JOSEPH SMITH, Jr.

KIRTLAND, OHIO:

PRINTED BY O. COWDERY & CO. FOR

P. P. PRATT AND J. GOODSON.

1837.

Title page of the second edition of the Book of Mormon, 1837.

THE SECOND EDITION, 1837

In so writing, they echoed the words of William W. Phelps, who was prevented by violence from printing the Book of Mormon in 1833. "The church of Christ has received the fulness of the gospel from the Book of Mormon," he wrote, "and every member as a true disciple of the blessed Savior, studies it as a heavenly treasure."[26]

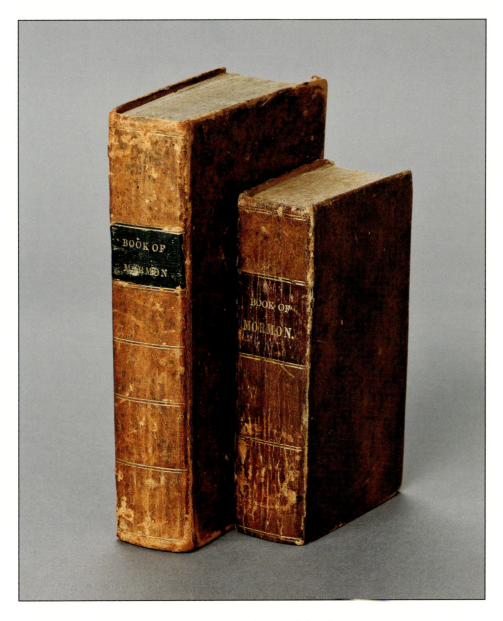

*First and second editions side by side;
the second edition (right) was deliberately sized to fit in a pocket.*

Cincinnati, Ohio, 1848. The third edition of the Book of Mormon was published here in 1840.

Chapter Five
THE THIRD EDITION, 1840

On March 14, 1838, Joseph Smith arrived in Far West, Missouri, which became the Church's new headquarters.[1] The apostasy of 1837 and 1838 swept Oliver Cowdery, William W. Phelps, and other men with scripture printing experience out of the Church, though Oliver and William later humbled themselves, repented, and were rebaptized.[2] A printing press bought by Oliver for the Kirtland print shop before his excommunication passed through several hands before it landed in Far West.[3]

The Mormon Missouri War erupted during the summer of 1838, resulting in some of the worst violence in Church history. On October 30, rogue Missouri militia attacked the peaceful Latter-day Saint village of Haun's Mill, massacring many men and boys and wounding others.[4] That night, as other militiamen besieged Far West, workers from the print shop buried the press and lead type to protect them.[5]

Far West soon fell, and Joseph Smith and other Church leaders were captured, chained, and imprisoned. After suffering the winter in a squalid jail in Liberty, Missouri, Joseph and his fellow prisoners escaped with the aid of their guards during a prisoner transfer. Soon arriving in Illinois, they joined other

Haun's Mill massacre.

Saints who had fled there for refuge, establishing a city called Nauvoo on a sweeping bend in the Mississippi River.[6]

In April 1839, as the last devout Saints were leaving Missouri, they dug up the printing press and type, hauling them to Illinois. That summer in Nauvoo, Joseph's brother Don Carlos and a printing partner, Ebenezer Robinson, set up temporary shop in a dank cellar and began cleaning the dirt-encrusted type. They had worked together in the Kirtland print shop, and in Nauvoo they built a new one and began printing a newspaper called *Times and Seasons*.[7]

In the December issue of the paper, they reported receiving many requests for books published by the Church. Regrettably, the scriptures and other works were "all disposed of." As a result, the First Presidency and high council of the Church voted "that the Book of Mormon be re-printed in this place, under the inspection of the Presidency, as soon as monies can be raised to defray the expenses."[8]

Nauvoo.

Ebenezer Robinson.

Getting money, however, was the challenge. As persecuted refugees who had lost their Missouri property, few Saints had means to lend.[9] In April 1840, Ebenezer and Don Carlos put an ad in the *Times and Seasons,* seeking to borrow a thousand dollars "to be appropriated to book printing."[10] Nothing happened. They tried again the next month, this time asking for half the amount.[11] Still no success.[12]

If only they could raise some money, they hoped to have the book typeset and ste-

Ad in the Times and Seasons.

reotyped in the east. Setting type for a large book was laborious and had to be repeated for each printing unless a mold was made of the set type and plates cast from it. The plate, called a stereotype, could be used to print copies when needed. Once the stereotyping was done, they could take the plates back to Nauvoo for printing.[13]

In late May, as Ebenezer entered the print shop, he had what he considered to be a divine manifestation. "It seemed that a ball of fire came down from above and striking the top of my head passed down into my heart," he said. It told him, "in plain and distinct language," just what to do to publish the Book of Mormon.

The inspiration was to have the book both stereotyped and printed in Cincinnati, Ohio. Normally, it would take months to create stereotype plates in Cincinnati and months more to print books from them once the plates reached Nauvoo. Now Ebenezer planned to begin printing pages in Cincinnati as soon as the first plate was finished. That way, most of the printing would already be finished when the last plate was made.[14]

They still needed money, but Ebenezer now knew how to solve that problem. He would send circulars to the branches of the Church, promising to send them 110 copies of the Book of Mormon for every hundred dollars they sent for printing. "God promised [me] that by the time we got the books out we would have money enough to pay for them," Ebenezer recalled. "From that minute I knew just what to do."[15]

Joseph Smith supported the plan and in June worked with Ebenezer to prepare a corrected text for publication. Comparing the first part of the printed text of the Book of Mormon to the original manuscript, they discovered some copying errors Oliver Cowdery had made in preparing the printer's manuscript. Joseph also made "a few additional emendations and grammatical changes."[16]

In 2 Nephi, for example, the 1830 and 1837 editions said the descendants of Book of Mormon people who accepted the gospel of Jesus Christ would become "a white and a delightsome people."[17] Joseph changed the verse to read that they would become "a pure and a delightsome people."[18] This was consistent with a Bible passage declaring that "man looketh on the outward appearance, but the Lord looketh on the heart."[19]

As a result of these changes, the title page of the new edition would carry the words, "Carefully Revised by the Translator."[20]

With a "God bless you" from Joseph, Ebenezer left for Cincinnati, taking an 1837 copy of the Book of Mormon with the corrections penciled in.[21] When he arrived there, he visited a stereotype foundry but had a bad feeling about it. At the next foundry, a man came forward and Ebenezer announced, "I have come to get the Book of Mormon stereotyped." At that, another man stepped up, saying, "When that book is stereotyped I am the man to stereotype it."[22]

They soon came to terms. Ebenezer offered to pay a hundred dollars he had on hand and the rest later. Even though they were total strangers, the businessman, Edwin Shepard, agreed. Shepard also introduced him to a book binder and to a paper vendor. "You are a stranger here, of course," the paper seller said, "and it them; wherefore, they shall be restored unto the knowledge of their fathers, and also to the knowledge of Jesus Christ, which was had among their fathers. And then shall they rejoice: for they shall know that it is a blessing unto them from the hand of God; and their scales of darkness shall begin to fall from their eyes; and many generations shall not pass away among them, save they shall be a (white) and a delightsome people.

shall be restored unto the knowledge of their fathers, and also to the knowledge of Jesus Christ, which was had among their fathers. And then shall they rejoice: for they shall know that it is a blessing unto them from the hand of God; and their scales of darkness shall begin to fall from their eyes; and many generations shall not pass away among them, save they shall be a (white) and a delightsome people.

they shall be restored unto the knowledge of their fathers, and also to the knowledge of Jesus Christ which was had among their fathers. And then shall they rejoice; for they shall know that it is a blessing unto them from the hand of God: and their scales of darkness shall begin to fall from their eyes: and many generations shall not pass away among them, save they shall be a (pure) and a delightsome people.

Top to bottom: 1830, 1837, and 1840 editions of the Book of Mormon. Note change of "white" to "pure" in the 1840 edition.

THE
BOOK OF MORMON.

AN ACCOUNT WRITTEN BY THE HAND OF MORMON UPON PLATES TAKEN FROM THE PLATES OF NEPHI.

Wherefore, it is an abridgment of the record of the people of Nephi, and also of the Lamanites; written to the Lamanites, who are a remnant of the house of Israel; and also to Jew and Gentile; written by way of commandment, and also by the spirit of prophecy and of revelation. Written, and sealed up, and hid up unto the Lord, that they might not be destroyed; to come forth by the gift and power of God unto the interpretation thereof; sealed by the hand of Moroni, and hid up unto the Lord, to come forth in due time by the way of Gentile; the interpretation thereof by the gift of God:

An abridgment taken from the book of Ether: also, which is a record of the people of Jared; who were scattered at the time the Lord confounded the language of the people, when they were building a tower to get to heaven: which is to shew unto the remnant of the house of Israel what great things the Lord hath done for their fathers; and that they may know the covenants of the Lord, that they are not cast off forever; and also to the convincing of the Jew and Gentile that Jesus is the Christ, the Eternal God, manifesting himself unto all nations. And now if there are faults, they are the mistakes of men; wherefore, condemn not the things of God, that ye may be found spotless at the judgment seat of Christ.

MORONI.

Book of Mormon, 1840 edition, attributing the language of the original title page to Moroni.

is customary to demand in such cases City references." Again Shepard spoke up, saying, "I am Mr. Robinson's backer."[23]

Miraculously, everything fell into place, just as Ebenezer felt it would, based on the manifestation he had in May. But events soon tested his faith. He stayed in Cincinnati to help with the project and to review page proofs to ensure accuracy of the stereotype plates. After paying Shepard the promised one hundred dollars, Ebenezer had almost nothing to live on. "My board bill was due and I had only a sixpence to go on," besides nine hundred dollars in new debt, "and it began to look a little blue," he remembered.[24]

He wrote to Don Carlos, who used the *Times and Seasons* to announce Ebenezer's success and "request all those, who feel an interest in the accomplishment of this glorious work, to assist in the arduous undertaking, by forwarding to him means to help defray the expences, which it requires in publishing a work of such magnitude." He promised a copy of the Book of Mormon, "well bound, for every dollar received in time to meet our engagements," with twenty bonus copies for those who sent a hundred dollars.[25]

Church leaders also called men to visit branches of the Church to raise money for the project. Soon funds flowed in to cover bills for the stereotyping, paper, printing, and binding on or before the day they were due. As copies of the book were finished, Ebenezer mailed them to subscribers. By the time he satisfied all the debts, he had a thousand copies of the Book of Mormon left over that could be sold. The project had been a remarkable success.[26]

"Books!!!" read the title of an article that Don Carlos ran in the July 1840 *Times and Seasons*. "The spread of truth for a few years past, has been so exceedingly rapid, that ... it has been impossible to keep the public supplied with books: and, inasmuch as the universal cry has been 'Books,' 'Books,' 'we want Books,' &c. and none could be had: we announce with pleasure, that effectual measures are now taking to accomplish the long desired object of getting books once more into circulation."

By buying copies of the new edition of the Book of Mormon, purchasers would provide funds for printing more books, thus opening "an effectual door" for spreading the desired word "before the world."[27]

During the October general conference in Nauvoo, the First Presidency announced "with great pleasure" that the new edition of the Book of Mormon had been printed and was soon expected to arrive from Cincinnati.[28] Ebenezer, who arrived back in the city the day before the meetings began, reported on his labors to the conference.[29]

By the end of October, the rest of the two thousand copies in the original printing had been shipped to Nauvoo.[30] In 1841 and 1842, Ebenezer reprinted perhaps another two thousand copies.[31] In 1841, his printing partner, Don Carlos Smith, died, and the following year, Ebenezer sold the printing establishment to the Church, assuring closer oversight of scripture publications.[32]

With the corrected stereotype plates in Church possession, Joseph Smith saw no reason to keep the original manuscript close at hand. On October 2, 1841, as the Nauvoo House hotel was being erected across the street from his home, he placed the manuscript in the building's cornerstone. Joseph reported first glimpsing the golden plates in a stone box in 1823. Now eighteen years later, with metal stereotype plates available, he sealed the Book of Mormon manuscript in a stone box to preserve it. It was the last time he saw it.[33]

Two months earlier, Joseph had also seen his brother Don Carlos for the last time. Before his death, Don Carlos had traveled to Cincinnati with Ebenezer Robinson to make the final payments to Edwin Shepard for the 1840 edition of the Book of Mormon. Once the debt was paid, Shepard bared his soul.

Cornerstone of the Nauvoo House in which Joseph Smith placed the original manuscript of the Book of Mormon in 1841.

THE
BOOK OF MORMON.

TRANSLATED BY
JOSEPH SMITH, Jr.

THIRD EDITION,
CAREFULLY REVISED BY THE TRANSLATOR.

NAUVOO, ILL:
PRINTED BY ROBINSON AND SMITH.
STEREOTYPED BY SHEPARD AND STEARNS,
West 3rd St. Cincinnati, Ohio.

1840.

Title page, Book of Mormon, third edition.

"Now," he asked, "do you want me to tell you why I did as I did when you came here last year?" He had risked his own financial security to help guarantee publication of the book. Putting his hand over his heart and turning to Ebenezer, he said, "I did it, not because of any thing that I saw in you, but because of what I felt in here."[34]

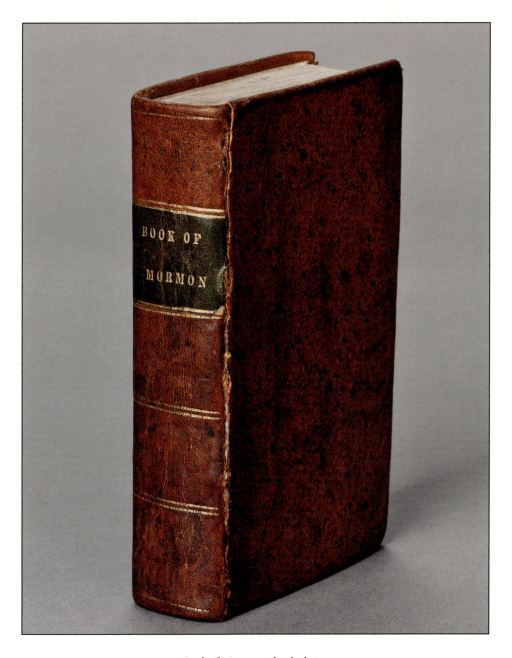

Book of Mormon, third edition.

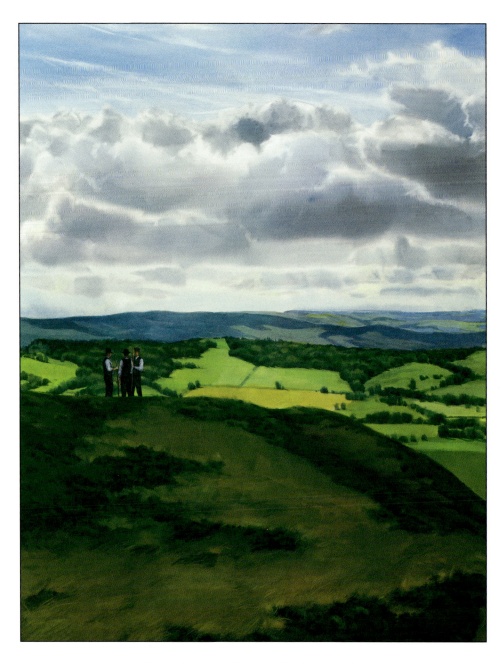

*Malvern Hills, England, with Herefordshire Beacon in the foreground,
where the decision was made to print the 1841 first European edition of the Book of Mormon.*

Chapter Six
THE FIRST EUROPEAN EDITION, 1841

On July 8, 1838, a few months after arriving in Far West and a month before the Missouri Mormon War broke out, Joseph Smith delivered a remarkable revelation in the name of the Lord. It directed members of the Church's Quorum of the Twelve Apostles "to go over the great waters" the next year as missionaries, taking leave of the Saints "on the twenty-sixth day of April next, on the building-spot of my house."[1]

The revelation boldly named a date and place for the missionaries' departure. After Far West fell and the refugee Saints fled toward Illinois, critics proclaimed this as one prophecy of Joseph Smith that would not be fulfilled. "The Twelve are now scattered all over creation," they boasted in Far West. "Let them come here if they dare; if they do, they will be murdered."[2]

The Twelve dared. In the early hours of April 26, 1839, Brigham Young and other apostles slipped undetected into Far West, held a meeting on the temple site, and took leave for their missions just as the revelation had instructed.[3]

They paused in the Nauvoo area to settle their families and receive instruction from Joseph Smith before moving on to England later in the year.[4]

Far West temple site where the Twelve met in 1839.

Since the 1840 Book of Mormon had not yet been printed, the most recent copy the missionaries could take with them was the 1837 Kirtland edition. It became the basis for the first volume of Latter-day Saint scripture published outside the United States: the 1841 first European (or fourth overall) edition of the Book of Mormon.[5]

Parley P. Pratt was an apostle who had a hand in publishing the 1837 edition. In New York on his way to England, he wrote to Joseph Smith, seeking permission for the Twelve to reprint the book. Joseph was away when the letter

Parley P. Pratt.

Brigham Young.

arrived, however, and his brother Hyrum answered it. Hyrum denied permission for printing the book in New York, but overseas was a different matter. When Joseph returned, Hyrum wrote, the Prophet would give the Twelve "full powers" to publish the Book of Mormon in England, "if it should be deemed wisdom."[6]

The first members of the Twelve to reach England held a conference in April 1840 and decided to seek a British copyright for the book.[7] Brigham Young sent the conference minutes to Joseph, asking for guidance if he saw "anything in or about the whole affair that is not right."[8]

Joseph would soon write two members of the Twelve who were still in Ohio, authorizing them to publish scriptures in Europe, as Hyrum had promised. In England, however, Brigham wouldn't get direction from Joseph on this matter for months. He didn't know for sure yet how Joseph felt. But he knew he had been sent to preach the gospel and that people clamored for the Book of Mormon.[9]

"It is all important to print immediately," Parley told Brigham, "for why withhold the fulness of the gospel, in the face of all the prophecies that it shall go to all nations?"[10]

"Shall we print the Book of Mormon in this country immediately?" Brigham wrote to Joseph on May 7. "They are calling for it from every quarter." Besides, he reasoned, custom duties on imported books were so high that "we need not think of bringing them from America."

"If I should act according to my feelings," Brigham said, "I should hand the Book of Mormon to this people as quickly as I could."[11]

On May 20, Brigham and others of the Twelve went to the Malvern Hills and climbed Herefordshire Beacon to pray and ponder. By the end of their experience, they felt God had directed them to proceed with publishing the Book of Mormon and to have Brigham Young spearhead the effort.[12]

In the days that followed, Brigham visited nearly every printer in Liverpool and Manchester, finally settling on Liverpool publisher John Tompkins & Company. Tompkins agreed to print five thousand copies of the Book of Mormon for £210, a bid £40 lower than the next closest one.[13]

The bid was low, and the work proved slow. When he signed contracts with Tompkins on June 17, Brigham optimistically expected the printing to be done in September. But it took until July 7 just to get paper for the project. The first printed sheets didn't reach the bindery until early January.[14]

Meanwhile, Brigham waited anxiously for some kind of confirmation from Joseph Smith that the Twelve had done right in moving forward with the book's publication. On September 5, 1840, Brigham coauthored a letter to Joseph and other members of the Church's First Presidency, asking, "Are we doing right in printing the Book of Mormon?" They also wondered, "When the Book of Mormon is completed, will it be best for any one to carry any of them to America?"

Brigham and the other missionaries hungered for direction. "Our motto is go ahead," the letter read. "Go ahead—& ahead we are determined to go—till we have conquered every foe. So come life or come death we'll go ahead, but tell us if we are going wrong & we will right it."[15]

On October 22, future apostle Lorenzo Snow arrived in Liverpool as a missionary. He carried with him a letter from Joseph Smith to the Twelve. By the time the letter had traveled from Nauvoo to New York and endured six weeks of stormy ocean travel, it was rather the worse for wear. Brigham had a tough time reading the smudged writing.

The message he got from the letter, however, grieved him. As best he could tell, Joseph was not happy that they had moved ahead without getting his explicit approval.[16]

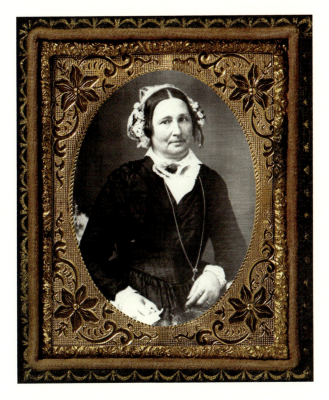

Mary Ann Young.

"All I have to say about the matter," Brigham wrote to his wife, Mary Ann, "is I have done all that I could to do good and promote the cause that we are in. I have done the very best that I knew how." He told her she could read the letter to Joseph "or not, just as you please, but tell him at any rate to say what he wants me to do and I will try and do it."[17]

On December 15, Joseph wrote to the Twelve again, answering their letter of September 5. "In my former epistle," he wrote, "I told you my mind respecting the printing of the Book of Mormon." Whether Brigham had correctly interpreted the earlier letter or not, Joseph was now pleased with the Twelve's efforts. He had learned that the Book of Mormon was printed, "which I am glad to hear," he wrote, "and should be pleased to hear that it was printed in all the different languages of the earth."[18]

> **BOOK OF MORMON.**
>
> This long looked for work is now out of press. The European edition consists of 5,000 copies, which we humbly trust will so far supply the public that they will now be able to peruse for themselves, a work which has been so grossly misrepresented; and which is in reality of more value to them than all the gold and silver of England. What heart can be so indifferent as not to wish to peruse the record of half a world? Bringing to light Gods dealings with them, together with their history of the past, and their prophesies of the future.— I repeat the declaration, strange as it may seem, that a knowledge of the things contained in this record is of more value to every one of them than the gold and silver of Europe.

Millennial Star *article announcing that a new edition of the Book of Mormon is available.*

Actually, the book was not quite finished when Joseph wrote his letter. Not until February 1841 did the Church's British newspaper, the *Millennial Star,* publish an article titled "Book of Mormon" that announced: "This long looked for work is now out of press. The European edition consists of 5,000 copies, which we humbly trust will so far supply the public that they will now be able to peruse for themselves, a work ... which is in reality of more value to them than all the gold and silver of England."[19]

The first copies were, in fact, finally available. But in the end, Tompkins, the printer, delivered only 4,050 of the promised copies before his company folded.[20] The company also refused to address complaints about pages left out when some of the books were bound.[21]

Still, the edition as a whole proved important in advancing missionary work in England.[22] It was also innovative, being the first to include an index as part of the book itself and to move the testimonies of the witnesses from the back to the front of the book. And, despite problems with the printing and binding, the edition became available in three grades of leather—morocco, calf, and sheep—in various colors, making it arguably the most beautifully bound edition published to date.[23]

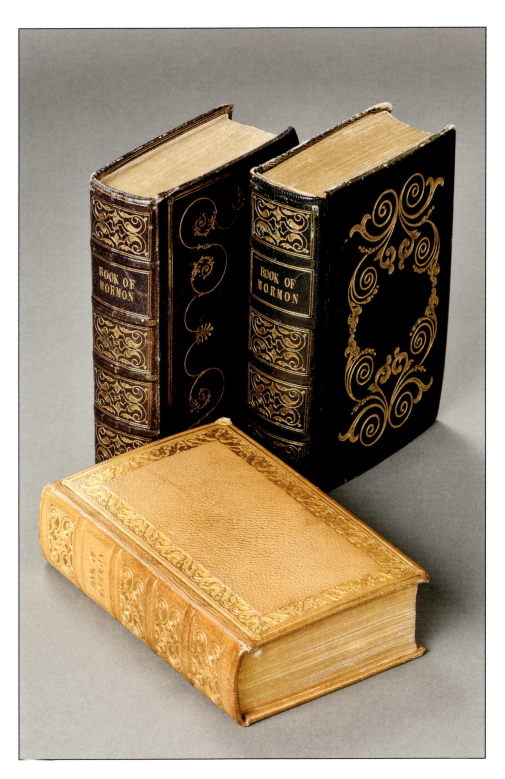

Variant bindings of the 1841 edition of the Book of Mormon.

Lorenzo Snow.

Heber C. Kimball.

Pleased with their accomplishment, Brigham Young and fellow apostle Heber C. Kimball sent copies of the book to each other's children as gifts.[24] Before leaving England in April 1841, Brigham also left "two neatly bound copies" for Lorenzo Snow, who had been appointed to preside over the Church in London. Through the good graces of Sir Henry Wheatley, Lorenzo presented them on Brigham's behalf to Queen Victoria and Prince Albert.[25]

Printed in gold on the front cover of the queen's book were the words, "To Queen Victoria, 1841," and on the back, "Presented by Brigham Young."[26]

Eliza R. Snow, Lorenzo's sister, later wrote a poem about the occasion, describing the queen's wealth and power. Two stanzas alluded to the Book of Mormon that Lorenzo presented:

> *But, lo! a prize possessing more*
> *Of worth than gems with honor rife—*
> *A herald of salvation bore*
> *To her the words of endless life.*
>
> *That gift, however fools deride,*
> *Is worthy of her royal care;*
> *She'd better lay her crown aside*
> *Than spurn the light reflected there.*[27]

Whether Queen Victoria ever read the book is unknown, but it became part of the Royal Library at Windsor Castle.[28]

The 1841 edition of the Book of Mormon also proved important in the history of scripture publication, though no one then knew just how important it would become. Because it followed the text of the 1837 Kirtland edition—though with British spellings—the 1841 Liverpool version lacked the corrections Joseph made in his Nauvoo edition of 1840, published during the Twelve's absence.[29]

Though another impression of the Book of Mormon was made in Nauvoo in 1842 from the plates used for the 1840 edition, the murder of Joseph Smith in 1844 and the driving of the Saints from Nauvoo in 1846 disrupted the printing of Latter-day Saint scriptures in America.[30] As a result, "it is from the Liverpool edition that all other LDS editions of the Book of Mormon descended."[31]

HER MOST GRACIOUS MAJESTY, QUEEN VICTORIA.
CABINET PORTRAIT

Liverpool, England. Verse numbers were first added to the edition of the Book of Mormon printed here in 1852.

Chapter Seven
CHAPTER AND VERSE

To be easily usable, the Book of Mormon needed to be divided into chapters and verses. Like the chapter and verse numbers in the Bible, those in the Book of Mormon were added or changed over time, making the scriptures simpler to cite.[1]

In dictating his original translation of the Book of Mormon, Joseph Smith apparently told his scribes to add the word *chapter* to the manuscript whenever he saw a narrative break in the text. Later, scribes went back and filled in the chapter numbers.[2]

In one case, a chapter number was changed in the original manuscript. When Martin Harris took the first 116 pages of the Book of Mormon to New York, they included not just the book of Lehi but apparently at least part of the first two chapters from the book of Mosiah. When Oliver Cowdery became scribe after the pages were lost, Joseph showed him part of Mosiah that Martin had transcribed but not taken with him. A revelation to Joseph about the loss of the 116 pages referred to it as "that which you have translated, which you have retained."[3]

The page was headed "Chapter III" in the original manuscript when Oliver received it, and he copied down "Chapter III" when he made the printer's manuscript. But because it was strange to begin a book with chapter 3, Oliver went back and changed "Chapter III" to "Chapter I."[4]

The original chapters of the Book of Mormon designated by Joseph Smith were much larger than the ones used in modern Latter-day Saint editions. For example, the book of Alma in the 1830 edition had thirty large chapters, compared to sixty-three smaller ones today. Because the chapters were large and the page numbers varied, depending on the edition, it was hard for teachers to point students to specific passages or for other publications to cite them.[5]

The problem was made worse by the fact that early editions of the Book of Mormon had no verse numbers. John H. Gilbert, who set type for the first edition, remembered with little exaggeration that in the Book of Mormon manuscript he used, "Every chapter . . . was one solid paragraph . . . from beginning to end."[6]

In the first edition, the chapters were broken into uneven, unnumbered paragraphs, some of which were very large.[7] Several paragraphs started on a page, continued over two more full pages, and ended on a fourth.[8] Four paragraphs reached to a fifth page.[9] The largest paragraph of all spanned eight pages.[10]

In addition, the fourth chapter in the book of Jacob was set as "one solid paragraph," as was the small last chapter in 3 Nephi and each of the first six chapters and last chapter in Moroni.[11]

Over time, these large paragraphs were broken down into smaller ones. The eight-page paragraph in the first edition of the Book of Mormon, for example, became two paragraphs in the second edition and remained that way for fifteen years.[12] Then in 1852, Franklin D. Richards of the Quorum of the Twelve broke those two paragraphs into a total of seven when he published an edition of the Book of Mormon in Liverpool, England.[13]

In that same 1852 edition, Elder Richards also took another step forward in

Franklin D. Richards.

THE BOOK OF MORMON:

AN ACCOUNT WRITTEN BY

THE HAND OF MORMON,

UPON

Plates taken from the Plates of Nephi.

Wherefore, it is an abridgment of the record of the people of Nephi, and also of the Lamanites; written to the Lamanites, who are a remnant of the House of Israel; and also to Jew and Gentile: written by way of commandment, and also by the spirit of prophecy and of revelation. Written and sealed up, and hid up unto the Lord, that they might not be destroyed; to come forth by the gift and power of God unto the interpretation thereof: sealed by the hand of Moroni, and hid up unto the Lord, to come forth in due time by the way of Gentile; the interpretation thereof by the gift of God:

An abridgment taken from the Book of Ether also; which is a record of the people of Jared; who were scattered at the time the Lord confounded the language of the people, when they were building a tower to get to heaven; which is to shew unto the remnant of the House of Israel what great things the Lord hath done for their fathers; and that they may know the covenants of the Lord, that they are not cast off for ever; and also to the convincing of the Jew and Gentile that JESUS is the CHRIST, the ETERNAL GOD, manifesting himself unto all nations. And now if there are faults, they are the mistakes of men; wherefore condemn not the things of God, that ye may be found spotless at the judgment-seat of Christ.   MORONI.

TRANSLATED BY JOSEPH SMITH, JUN.

Third European Edition.

STEREOTYPED.

Liverpool:
PUBLISHED BY F. D. RICHARDS, 15, WILTON STREET.
London:
SOLD AT THE L. D. SAINTS' BOOK DEPOT,
35, JEWIN STREET;
AND BY ALL BOOKSELLERS.

1852.

Title page of the third European edition of the Book of Mormon.
This was the first edition to have verse numbers.

making the book easier to use. He decided to number the paragraphs in the volume and thus became the first person to add verse numbers to the Book of Mormon.[14]

Now, for the first time, people could cite the Book of Mormon in the same way they did the Bible: by chapter and verse instead of edition and page number. But even with Elder Richards's numbering system, finding specific phrases in the Book of Mormon was not always easy because the verses remained relatively large. When a verse spanned multiple pages, teachers still had to cite page numbers to guide students.

The next major step came in 1879 when Orson Pratt of the Quorum of the Twelve finally divided the large chapters and numbered paragraphs into small chapters and small verses.[15] Under Orson Pratt's system, Mormon 4:1–7 in the 1852 edition, which spanned seven pages, became seventy-two verses in the 1879 edition: Mormon 8:1–9:31.[16] Other large paragraphs throughout the book were also broken into small verses that made for easier citation.

With these changes, leaders, teachers, parents, and missionaries had no trouble in quickly directing listeners or readers to passages. As a result, the numbering system in the 1879 edition became the standard used in later Latter-day Saint editions of the Book of Mormon.[17]

Orson Pratt.

THE BOOK OF MORMON:

AN ACCOUNT WRITTEN BY

THE HAND OF MORMON,

UPON

Plates taken from the Plates of Nephi.

Wherefore it is an abridgment of the record of the people of Nephi, and also of the Lamanites; written to the Lamanites who are a remnant of the house of Israel; and also to Jew and Gentile: written by way of commandment, and also by the Spirit of prophecy and of revelation. Written and sealed up, and hid up unto the Lord, that they might not be destroyed; to come forth by the gift and power of God unto the interpretation thereof: sealed by the hand of Moroni, and hid up unto the Lord, to come forth in due time by the way of Gentile; the interpretation thereof by the gift of God.

An abridgment taken from the Book of Ether also; which is a record of the people of Jared; who were scattered at the time the Lord confounded the language of the people when they were building a tower to get to heaven; which is to shew unto the remnant of the House of Israel what great things the Lord hath done for their fathers; and that they may know the covenants of the Lord, that they are not cast off forever; and also to the convincing of the Jew and Gentile that JESUS is the CHRIST, the ETERNAL GOD, manifesting himself unto all nations. And now if there are faults, they are the mistakes of men: wherefore condemn not the things of God, that ye may be found spotless at the judgment-seat of Christ.

TRANSLATED BY JOSEPH SMITH, JUN.

DIVISION INTO CHAPTERS AND VERSES, WITH REFERENCES,

BY ORSON PRATT, SEN.

ELECTROTYPE EDITION.

LIVERPOOL:

PRINTED AND PUBLISHED BY WILLIAM BUDGE, 42, ISLINGTON.

1879.

As the title page explains, Orson Pratt divided the text of the Book of Mormon into smaller chapters and verses for the 1879 edition.

have been commanded of my father. And now it came to pass that after the great and tremendous battle at Camorah, behold, the Nephites which had escaped into the country southward, were hunted by the Lamanites, until they were all destroyed; and my father also was killed by them; and I, even I remaineth alone to write the sad tale of the destruction of my people. But behold, they are gone, and I fulfil the commandment of my father. And whether they will slay me, I know not; therefore I will write and hide up the records in the earth: and whither I go it mattereth not. Behold, my father hath made this record, and he hath written the intent thereof. And behold, I would write it also, if I had room upon the plates; but I have not. Friends I have none, for I am alone: my father hath been slain in battle, and all my kinsfolks, and I have not friends nor whither to go; and how long that the Lord will suffer that I may live, I know not. Behold, four hundred years have passed away since the coming of our Lord and Saviour. And behold, the Lamanites have hunted my people, the Nephites, down from city to city, and from place to place, even until they are no more; and great has been their fall; yea, great and marvellous is the destruction of my people, the Nephites. And behold, it is the hand of the Lord which hath done it. And behold also, the Lamanites are at war one with another; and the whole face of this land is one continual round of murder and bloodshed; and no one knoweth the end of the war. And now behold, I say no more concerning them, for there are none, save it be Lamanites and robbers, that do exist upon the face of the land; and there are none that do know the true God, save it be the disciples of Jesus, which did tarry in the land until the wickedness of the people were so great, that the Lord would not suffer them to remain with the people; and whether they be upon the face of the land, no man knoweth. But behold, my father and I have seen them, and they have ministered unto us. And whoso receiveth this record, and shall not condemn it because of the imperfections which are in it, the same shall know of greater things than these. Behold, I am Moroni; and were it possible, I would make all things known unto you. Behold, I make an end of speaking concerning this people. I am the son of Mormon, and my father was a descendant of Nephi; and I am the same which hideth up this record unto the Lord; the plates thereof are of no worth, because of the commandment of the Lord. For he truly saith, That no one

Page 532 from the first edition.
The huge paragraph, part of which is shown here, spans eight pages of the book.

dirt out of the ditch against the breastwork of timbers; and thus they did cause the Lamanites to labor, until they had encircled the city of Bountiful round about with a strong wall of timbers and earth, to an exceeding height. And this city became an exceeding strong hold ever after; and in this city they did guard the prisoners of the Lamanites; yea, even within a wall, which they had caused them to build with their own hands. Now Moroni was compelled to cause the Lamanites to labor, because it were easy to guard them while at their labor; and he desired all his forces, when he should make an attack upon the Lamanites.

And it came to pass that Moroni had thus gained a victory over one of the greatest of the armies of the Lamanites, and had obtained possession of the city Mulek, which was one of the strongest holds of the Lamanites in the land of Nephi; and thus he had also built a strong hold to retain his prisoners. And it came to pass that he did no more attempt a battle with the Lamanites in that year, but he did employ his men in preparing for war; yea, and in making fortifications to guard against the Lamanites; yea, and also delivering their women and their children from famine and affliction, and providing food for their armies.

And now it came to pass that the armies of the Lamanites, on the West Sea, south, while in the absence of Moroni, on account of some intrigue amongst the Nephites, which caused dissensions amongst them, had gained some ground over the Nephites, yea, insomuch that they had obtained possession of a number of their cities in that part of the land; and thus because of iniquity amongst themselves, yea, because of dissensions and intrigue among themselves, they were placed in the most dangerous circumstances.

And now behold, I have somewhat to say concerning the people of Ammon, which, in the beginning, were Lamanites; but by Ammon and his brethren, or rather by the power and word of God, they had been converted unto the Lord; and they had been brought down into the land of Zarahemla, and had ever since been protected by the Nephites; and because of their oath, they had been kept from taking up arms against their brethren: for they had taken an oath, that they never would shed blood more; and according to their oath, they would have perished; yea, they would have suffered themselves to have fallen into the hands of their brethren, had it

Page 375 from the 1830 edition of the Book of Mormon.
Note the unnumbered paragraphs.

358   BOOK OF ALMA.   [CHAP. XXIV.

Bountiful; and he caused that they should build a breastwork of timbers upon the inner bank of the ditch; and they cast up dirt out of the ditch against the breastwork of timbers; and thus they did cause the Lamanites to labor until they had encircled the city of Bountiful round about with a strong wall of timbers and earth, to an exceeding height. And this city became an exceeding strong hold ever after; and in this city they did guard the prisoners of the Lamanites; yea, even within a wall, which they had caused them to build with their own hands. Now Moroni was compelled to cause the Lamanites to labor, because it were easy to guard them while at their labor: and he desired all his forces, when he should make an attack upon the Lamanites.

17. And it came to pass that Moroni had thus gained a victory over one of the greatest of the armies of the Lamanites, and had obtained possession of the city of Mulek, which was one of the strongest holds of the Lamanites in the Land of Nephi; and thus he had also built a strong hold to retain his prisoners. And it came to pass that he did no more attempt a battle with the Lamanites in that year, but he did employ his men in preparing for war; yea, and in making fortifications to guard against the Lamanites; yea, and also delivering their women and their children from famine and affliction, and providing food for their armies.

18. And now it came to pass that the armies of the Lamanites, on the West sea, south, while in the absence of Moroni, on account of some intrigue amongst the Nephites, which caused dissensions amongst them, had gained some ground over the Nephites, yea, insomuch that they had obtained possession of a number of their cities in that part of the land; and thus because of iniquity amongst themselves, yea, because of dissensions and intrigue among themselves, they were placed in the most dangerous circumstances.

19. And now behold, I have somewhat to say concerning the people of Ammon, who, in the beginning, were Lamanites; but by Ammon and his brethren, or rather by the power and word of God, they had been converted unto the Lord: and they had been brought down into the land of Zarahemla, and had ever since been protected by the Nephites; and because of their oath, they had been kept from taking up arms against their brethren; for they had taken an oath, that they never would shed blood more; and according to their oath they would have perished; yea, they would have suffered themselves to have fallen into the hands of their brethren, had it not been for the pity and the exceeding love which Ammon and his

The same text from the 1852 edition, showing paragraph numbers added by Franklin D. Richards.

have rejected the prophets, and your rulers, and the seers hath he covered because of your iniquity.

17. And it shall come to pass, that the Lord God shall bring forth unto you the words of a book, and they shall be the words of them which have slumbered. And behold the book shall be sealed : and in the book shall be a revelation from God, from the beginning of the world to the ending thereof. Wherefore, because of the things which are sealed up, the things which are sealed shall not be delivered in the day of the wickedness and abominations of the people. Wherefore the book shall be kept from them. But the book shall be delivered unto a man, and he shall deliver the words of the book, which are the words of those who have slumbered in the dust; and he shall deliver these words unto another; but the words which are sealed he shall not deliver, neither shall he deliver the book. For the book shall be sealed by the power of God, and the revelation which was sealed shall be kept in the book until the own due time of the Lord, that they may come forth . for behold, they reveal all things from the foundation of the world unto the end thereof. And the day cometh that the words of the book which were sealed shall be read upon the house tops; and they shall be read by the power of Christ: and all things shall be revealed unto the children of men which ever have been among the children of men, and which ever will be, even unto the end of the earth. Wherefore, at that day when the book shall be delivered unto the man of whom 1 have spoken, the book shall be hid from the eyes of the world, that the eyes of none shall behold it save it be that three witnesses shall behold it, by the power of God, besides him to whom the book shall be delivered; and they shall testify to the truth of the book and the things therein. And there is none other which shall view it, save it be a few, according to the will of God, to bear testimony of his word unto the children of men: for the Lord God hath said, that the words of the faithful should speak as if it were from the dead. Wherefore, the Lord God will proceed to bring forth the words of the book; and in the mouth of as many witnesses as seemeth him good, will he establish his word ; and wo be unto him that rejecteth the word of God.

18. But behold, it shall come to pass that the Lord God shall say unto him to whom he shall deliver the book, take these words which are not sealed and deliver them to another, that he may shew them unto the learned, saying, read this, I pray thee. And the learned shall say, bring hither the

Page 102 from the 1852 edition, showing a full-page paragraph.

shall be unto them, even as unto a hungry man, which dreameth, and behold he eateth, but he awaketh and his soul is empty; or like unto a thirsty man, which dreameth, and behold he drinketh, but he awaketh, and behold he is faint, and his soul hath appetite: yea, even so shall the multitude of all the nations be that fight against Mount Zion:

4. For behold, all ye that do iniquity, stay yourselves and wonder, for ye shall cry out, and cry; yea, ye shall be drunken, but not with wine, ye shall stagger, but not with strong drink:

5. For behold, the Lord hath poured out upon you the spirit of deep sleep. For behold, ye have closed your eyes, and ye have rejected the prophets; and your rulers, and the seers hath he covered because of your iniquity.

6. And it shall come to pass, that the Lord God shall bring forth unto you the words of a ^{c}book, and they shall be the words of them which have slumbered.

7. And behold the book shall be ^{d}sealed: and in the book shall be a ^{e}revelation from God, from the beginning of the world to the ending thereof.

8. Wherefore, because of the things which are sealed up, the things which are sealed shall not be delivered in the ^{f}day of the wickedness and abominations of the people. Wherefore the book shall be kept from them.

9. But the book shall be delivered unto a ^{g}man, and he shall deliver the words of the book, which are the words of those who have slumbered in the dust; and he shall deliver these words unto ^{h}another;

10. But the words which are sealed he shall not deliver, neither shall he deliver the book. For the book shall be sealed by the power of God, and the revelation which was sealed shall be kept in the book until the own ^{i}due time of the Lord, that they may come forth: for behold, they ^{j}reveal all things from the foundation of the world unto the end thereof.

11. And the day cometh that the words of the book which were sealed shall be read upon the house tops; and they shall be read by the power of Christ: and all things shall be ^{k}revealed unto the children of men which ever have been among the children of men, and which ever will be, even unto the end of the earth.

12. Wherefore, at that day when the book shall be delivered unto the ^{l}man of whom I have spoken, the book shall be hid from the eyes of the world, that the eyes of none shall behold it save it be that ^{m}three witnesses shall behold it, by the power of God, besides him to whom the

c, I. Nep. 13: 34, 35, 39—42. II. Nep. 3: 6—23. 26: 16, 17. 29: 11. Enos 1: 13—18. Mor. 5: 12, 13. 8: 14—16, 25—32. *d*, Isa. 29: 11. *e*, Ether 4: 1—7. *f*, Ether 4: 6, 7. *g*, Joseph Smith, Jr. *h*, Martin Harris. *i*, Ether 4: 7, 15. *j*, Ether 4: 15. *k*, Ether 4: 6, 7, 13—17. *l*, Joseph Smith, Jr. *m*, see *c*, II. Nep. 11.

Page 114 from the 1879 edition, showing the same paragraph broken into verses.

*The Church Administration Building, Salt Lake City,
where the 1920 edition of the Book of Mormon was developed.*

Chapter Eight
THE 1920 EDITION

After the 1879 edition prepared by Orson Pratt, the next major English edition of the Book of Mormon appeared in 1920. It was produced by a committee of apostles, chaired by George F. Richards, that included Anthony W. Ivins, Joseph Fielding Smith, James E. Talmage, and Melvin J. Ballard. The combined gospel scholarship of these men resulted in an edition of the Book of Mormon that made scripture study simpler and more effective.[1]

One change these men made was to further standardize the titles of the four books whose authors were named Nephi. In the 1830 edition, these books were titled "The First Book of Nephi"; "The Second Book of Nephi"; "The Book of Nephi, the Son of Nephi, Which Was the Son of Helaman"; and "The Book of Nephi, Which Is the Son of Nephi, One of the Disciples of Jesus Christ."[2]

The second edition (1837) changed the word "Which" to "Who" in the titles of the latter two books, which then became "The Book of Nephi, the Son of Nephi, Who Was the Son of Helaman," and "The Book of Nephi, Who Is the Son of Nephi, One of the Disciples of Jesus Christ."[3]

Orson Pratt's 1879 edition had made citation easier by adding the words "III. Nephi" and "IV. Nephi" to the beginning of the latter two books' titles, respectively.[4] Some subsequent editions replaced the Roman numerals "III" and "IV" with Arabic numerals, resulting in "3 Nephi" and "4 Nephi."[5] These numerals could be read as either cardinal or ordinal numbers. For example, "III. Nephi" could be read "Three Nephi" or "Third Nephi."

> **THE BOOK OF NEPHI,**
>
> THE SON OF NEPHI, WHICH WAS THE SON OF HELAMAN.
>
> **CHAPTER I.**
>
> *And Helaman was the son of Helaman, which was the son of Alma, which was the son of Alma, being a descendant of Nephi, which was the son of Lehi, which came out of Jerusalem in the first year of the reign of Zedekiah, the king of Judah.*

> III. NEPHI.
>
> **THE BOOK OF NEPHI,**
>
> THE SON OF NEPHI, WHO WAS THE SON OF HELAMAN.
>
> *And Helaman was the son of Helaman, who was the son of Alma, who was the son of Alma, being a descendant of Nephi who was the son of Lehi, who came out of Jerusalem in the first year of the reign of Zedekiah, the king of Judah.*

> **THIRD NEPHI**
> **THE BOOK OF NEPHI**
>
> THE SON OF NEPHI, WHO WAS THE SON OF HELAMAN
>
> *And Helaman was the son of Helaman, who was the son of Alma, who was the son of Alma, being a descendant of Nephi who was the son of Lehi, who came out of Jerusalem in the first year of the reign of Zedekiah, the king of Judah.*

Top to bottom: 1830, 1879, and 1920 editions of the Book of Mormon. Note changes in the title at the top of each page.

188 BOOK OF MOSIAH. [CHAP. XII.

21. And except they repent, and turn to the Lord their God, behold, I will deliver them into the hands of their enemies: yea, and they shall be brought into *ᵘbondage*; and they shall be afflicted by the hand of their enemies.

22. And it shall come to pass that they shall know that I am the Lord their God, and am a jealous God, visiting the iniquities of my people.

23. And it shall come to pass that except this people repent, and turn unto the Lord their God, they shall be brought into *ᵛbondage*: and none shall deliver them, except it be the Lord the Almighty God.

24. Yea, and it shall come to pass that when they shall cry unto me, I will be *ʷslow* to hear their cries; yea, and I will suffer them that they be smitten by their enemies.

25. And except they repent in sackcloth and ashes, and cry mightily to the Lord their God, I will not hear their prayers, neither will I deliver them out of their afflictions; and thus saith the Lord, and thus hath he commanded me.

26. Now it came to pass that when Abinadi had spoken these words unto them, they were wroth with him, and sought to take away his life; but the Lord delivered him out of their hands.

27. Now when king Noah had heard of the words which Abinadi had spoken unto the people, he was also wroth; and he said, Who is Abinadi, that I and my people should be judged of him? or who is the Lord, that shall bring upon my people such great affliction?

28. I command you to bring Abinadi hither, that I may slay him: for he has said these things that he might stir up my people to anger one with another, and to raise contentions among my people; therefore I will slay him.

29. Now the eyes of the people were blinded: therefore they hardened their hearts against the words of Abinadi, and they sought from that time forward to take him. And king Noah hardened his heart against the word of the Lord, and he did not repent of his evil doings.

CHAPTER 12.

1. And it came to pass that after the space of two years, that Abinadi came among them in disguise, that they knew him not, and began to prophesy among them, saying, Thus has the Lord commanded me, saying: Abinadi, go and prophesy unto this my people, for they have hardened their hearts against my words: they have repented not of their evil doings; therefore, I will visit them in my anger, yea, in my fierce anger will I visit them in their iniquities and abominations;

---

u, ver. 23. See *k*, Mos. 9. 12: 2.   *v*, see *u*.   *w*, ver. 25. Mos. 21: 14, 15.

Early copies of the Book of Mormon, such as the 1879 edition shown here, were printed in a single-column format.

158 MOSIAH, 12.

CHAPTER 12.

Abinadi, for denouncing evil-doers, is cast into prison—The false priests sit in judgment upon him—They are confounded.

1. And it came to pass that *after the space of two years that Abinadi came among them in disguise, that they knew him not, and began to prophesy among them, saying: Thus has the Lord commanded me, saying—Abinadi, go and prophesy unto this my people, for they have hardened their hearts against my words; they have repented not of their evil doings; therefore, I will visit them in my anger, yea, in my fierce anger will I visit them in their iniquities and abominations.

2. Yea, wo be unto this generation! And the Lord said unto me: Stretch forth thy hand and prophesy, saying: Thus saith the Lord, it shall come to pass that this generation, because of their iniquities, shall be brought into ^abondage, and shall be smitten ^bon the cheek; yea, and shall be driven ^cby men, and shall be slain; and the vultures of the air, and the dogs, yea, and the wild beasts, shall devour their flesh.

3. And it shall come to pass that the life of king Noah shall be valued even as a ^dgarment in a hot furnace; for he shall know that I am the Lord.

4. And it shall come to pass that I will smite this my people with sore afflictions, yea, with famine and with pestilence; and I will cause that they shall ^ehowl all the day long.

5. Yea, and I will cause that they shall have burdens ^flashed upon their backs; and they shall be driven before like a dumb ass.

6. And it shall come to pass that I will send forth hail among them, and it shall smite them; and they shall also be smitten with the ^geast wind; and insects shall pester their land also, and devour their grain.

7. And they shall be smitten with a great pestilence—and all this will I do because of their iniquities and abominations.

8. And it shall come to pass that except they repent I will ^hutterly destroy them from off the face of the earth; yet they shall ⁱleave a record behind them, and I will preserve them for ^jother nations which shall possess the land; yea, even this will I do that I may discover the abominations of this people to other nations. And many things did Abinadi prophesy against this people.

9. And it came to pass that they were angry with him; and they took him and carried him bound before the king, and said unto the king: Behold, we have brought a man before thee who has prophesied evil concerning thy people, and saith that God will destroy them.

10. And he also prophesieth evil concerning thy life, and saith that thy life shall be as a ^kgarment in a furnace of fire.

11. And again, he saith that thou shalt be as a stalk, even as a dry stalk of the field, which is run over by the beasts and trodden under foot.

12. And again, he saith thou shalt be as the blossoms of a thistle, which, when it is fully ripe, if the wind bloweth, it is driven forth upon the face of the land. And he pretendeth the Lord hath spoken it. And he saith all this

---

a, see *u*, Mos. 11. *b*, Mos. 21:3. *c*, ver. 5. Mos. 21:3, 4, 13. *d*, Mos. 19:20. *e*, Mos. 21:1—15. *f*, Mos. 21:3. *g*, Mos. 7:31. *h*, 1 Ne. 12:19. 2 Ne. 26:10, 11. Al. 45:9—14. He. 13:5, 6. 3 Ne. 27:32. Morm. 6. *i*, Morm. 8:14—16. See *c*, 2 Ne. 27. *j*, see *s*, 1 Ne. 13. *k*, ver. 3. * ABOUT B. C. 148.

The 1920 edition divided the text into two columns, as did many Bibles of the period.

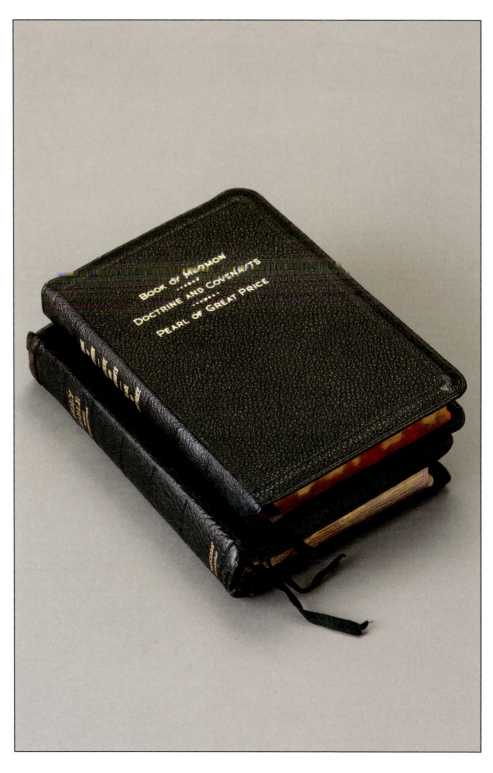

*Once the Book of Mormon began to appear in a double-column format,
it was frequently published in bindings matching a Church-approved Bible.*

To eliminate the ambiguity, the 1920 scriptures committee standardized the book names to "Third Nephi" and "Fourth Nephi," the words "Third" and "Fourth" being grammatically consistent with "First" and "Second" in the names of the first two books of Nephi.[6] They also made other grammatical changes, continuing the tradition of updating the language to make it more consistent with that of many modern readers.[7]

For centuries, Bibles—including the Gutenberg Bible of the 1450s and the King James Version of 1611—had been printed in a double-column format.[8] The 1920 edition of the Book of Mormon presented the text in double-column format for the first time, making the texts of the Bible and the Book of Mormon appear even more similar.[9] This, in turn, led to the frequent binding of the Bible and other Latter-day Saint scriptures as sets in matching leather, the Bible often being a King James Version that was approved by the Church and furnished by Cambridge University Press.[10]

Yet another change in the 1920 edition was the introduction of chapter summaries. The scribes for the original manuscript of the Book of Mormon sometimes wrote a short heading at the top of a manuscript page after filling it with Joseph Smith's dictation. But the printer's manuscript omitted those headings. They, of course, were not part of the text Joseph dictated from the golden plates.[11]

Today, however, at the front of some books in the Book of Mormon—and in the middle of others—summaries appear that were part of the dictated text. The Second Book of Nephi, for example, begins as follows:

> *An account of the death of Lehi. Nephi's brethren rebel against him. The Lord warns Nephi to depart into the wilderness. His journeyings in the wilderness, and so forth.*

This summary appears in the original Book of Mormon manuscript.[12]

Another example occurs between the current chapters 22 and 23 of the book of Mosiah:

An account of Alma and the people of the Lord, who were driven into the wilderness by the people of King Noah.

This too is a part of the original text of the Book of Mormon, though the words that follow—"Comprising chapters 23 and 24"—were added later, after the small chapter system of the book was adopted.[13]

The members of the 1920 scriptures committee added a short summary to the beginning of each chapter in the Book of Mormon. These headings, with some changes, were also grouped together at the back of the book in a section titled "Synopsis of Chapters."[14]

Besides standardizing the titles of the four books of Nephi, the 1920 scriptures committee included another innovation in the new edition: a "Pronouncing Vocabulary."[15] The Book of Mormon contains 337 proper names, more than half of which are unique to the volume.[16] Without a standard to guide them, readers pronounced the names in different ways.

To help solve that problem, Church president Joseph F. Smith agreed to appoint a committee at Brigham Young University in 1903 to develop rules for pronunciation, "provided," he joked to the committee members, "you do not afterwards cut me off [from] the Church if I don't pronounce the words according to the rule adopted by the committee." The committee suggested arbitrary but uniform rules for pronunciation to aid readers.[17]

Eventually, the Deseret Sunday School Union Board (predecessor of the general Sunday School presidency) established another group to further the work of the 1903 committee. It came up with a "Pronouncing Vocabulary" that was first published in 1910 in George Reynolds's *A Dictionary of the Book of Mormon*.[18]

3 NEPHI, 1.

which they did, Satan did get great hold upon the hearts of the people upon all the face of the land.

24. And thus *ended the nine- tieth year of the reign of the judges over the people of Nephi.

25. And thus ended the book of Helaman, according to the record of Helaman and his sons.

THIRD NEPHI
THE BOOK OF NEPHI

THE SON OF NEPHI, WHO WAS THE SON OF HELAMAN

And Helaman was the son of Helaman, who was the son of Alma, who was the son of Alma, being a descendant of Nephi who was the son of Lehi, who came out of Jerusalem in the first year of the reign of Zedekiah, the king of Judah.

CHAPTER 1

Nephi, son of Helaman, departs—Signs given of the Savior's birth—Opposite effects manifest—Again, the Gadianton band.

1. Now it came to pass that the †ninety and first year had passed away and it was ^{a}six hundred years from the time that Lehi left Jerusalem; and it was in the year that Lachoneus was the chief judge and the governor over the land.

2. And Nephi, the son of Helaman, had departed out of the land of ^{b}Zarahemla, giving charge unto his son Nephi, who was his eldest son, concerning the ^{c}plates of brass, and all the records which had been kept, and ^{d}all those things which had been kept sacred from the departure of Lehi out of Jerusalem.

3. Then he departed out of the land, and ^{e}whither he went, no man knoweth; and his son Nephi did keep the records in his stead, yea, the record of this people.

4. And it came to pass that in the commencement of the ninety and second year, behold, the prophecies of the prophets began to be fulfilled more fully; for there began to be ^{f}greater signs and greater miracles wrought among the people.

5. But there were some who began to say that the time was past for the words to be fulfilled, which were ^{g}spoken by Samuel, the Lamanite.

6. And they began to rejoice over their brethren, saying: Behold the time is past, and the words of Samuel are not fulfilled; therefore, your joy and your faith concerning this thing hath been vain.

7. And it came to pass that they did make a great uproar throughout the land; and the people who believed began to be very sorrowful, lest by any means those things which had been spoken might not come to pass.

8. But behold, they did watch steadfastly ^{h}for that day and that night and that day which should be as one day as if there were no night, that they might know that their faith had not been vain.

9. Now it came to pass that there was a day set apart by the unbelievers, that all those who be-

---

a, 1 Ne. 10:4. *b*, Om. 13. *c*, see *a*, 1 Ne. 3. *d*, Al. 37. *e*, 3 Ne. 2:9. *f*, He. 16:13, 23. *g*, He. 14:2—7. *h*, He. 14:3, 4. * B. C. 1. † A. D. 1.

The first page of Third Nephi in the 1920 edition of the Book of Mormon. The italicized paragraph just below the book's title was part of the original dictated text. The summary under "Chapter 1" was added by the 1920 scriptures committee.

the rebels—Help sent to Helaman, Lehi, and Teancum—Lamanites concentrate in land of Moroni—Teancum slays Ammoron, at cost of his own life—Lamanites driven out of the land 353

Chap. 63—Shiblon succeeds Helaman—Death of Moroni—Hagoth, builder of ships—Nephite voyages to the land northward—Helaman, son of Helaman, keeps the records—Moronihah defeats Lamanites—End of Alma's account 358

THE BOOK OF HELAMAN

Chap. 1—Pahoran's sons contend for the judgment-seat—Pahoran the second is murdered by Kishkumen—Coriantumr, Nephite dissenter, is leader of the Lamanites—Zarahemla captured and retaken 359

Chap. 2—Helaman the second is appointed chief judge—Kishkumen slain by Helaman's servant—Secret combinations—The Gadianton robbers escape 362

Chap. 3—More migrations to the north—A land of large waters—Buildings of cement—Many records kept—Helaman dies—His son, Nephi, succeeds him 363

Chap. 4—Many dissensions in the church—Lamanites again invade land of Zarahemla—The city captured—Nephites driven into the land Bountiful—Moronihah fortifies the way—Weakened by wickedness, the Nephites prevail not 366

Chap. 5—Nephi yields judgment-seat to Cezoram—With his brother Lehi he devotes himself to the ministry—Marvelous manifestations—Converted Lamanites restore conquered Nephite lands 368

Chap. 6—Lamanites send missionaries to Nephites—Peace and freedom abound—The land Lehi and the land Mulek—Cezoram murdered—His son also murdered—Gadianton robbers seize government 372

Chap. 7—Beginning of the prophecy of Nephi, son of Helaman—Nephi, rejected by the people in the north, returns to Zarahemla—From his garden tower he prays to God and addresses the multitude 376

Chap. 8—Nephi's address continued—Corrupt judges vainly endeavor to incite people against him—By inspiration he announces the murder of the chief judge 378

Chap. 9—Nephi's words verified—Chief judge found dead at the judgment-seat—Nephi and five others accused—Their innocence established—The murderer made known................ 380

Chap. 10—Nephi is comforted by the Lord with promise of great power—He preaches repentance and warns the wicked of impending judgments... 383

Chap. 11—Further depredations by the secret band of robbers—A great famine—The famishing people turn to the Lord and are again prospered—Dissension and strife follow—The Gadianton band more active................... 385

Chap. 12—Mormon's commentary on the condition of the people—Human frailty and the goodness and power of God—Blessed are the penitent—Men to be judged according to their works.. 388

Chap. 13—Beginning of the prophecy of Samuel the Lamanite—Samuel proclaims his prophecies from the city wall—Sword of justice to fall on fourth generation—Nephite cities spared for sake of the righteous—Land to be cursed—Slippery treasures.......... 389

Chap. 14—Samuel the Lamanite predicts the Christ—The signs of Christ's birth to be given in five years—Signs of his death also foretold.............. 393

Chap. 15—Samuel the Lamanite continues his warning words—A remnant of his people to be preserved—Nephites to be utterly destroyed unless they repent 395

Chap. 16—Some of the Nephites join the church of Christ—The majority reject Samuel's testimony—They attempt to assault and bind him—He escapes and returns to his own country—Nephi's further ministry—Skepticism abounds 397

THIRD NEPHI

Chap. 1—Nephi, son of Helaman, departs—Signs of the Savior's birth actually appear—Opposite effects manifest—Again, the Gadianton band........ 399

Chap. 2—Nephite degeneracy — Nephite reckoning of time changed—White Lamanites—Both peoples unite for defence against the bands of robbers and murderers 401

Chap. 3—Lachoneus, governor of the land, receives epistle from Gaddianhi, the robber chieftain—Surrender demanded—Lachoneus ignores demand and prepares for defence........... 403

Chap. 4—The robbers beaten and their leader slain—His successor, Zemnarihah, hanged—Gidgiddoni's military prowess 406

Chap. 5—Nephites repent and seek to end works of wickedness—Mormon's account of himself and of the plates kept by him—Another allusion to the gathering of Israel................. 408

Chap. 6—The people are prospered—Pride, wealth, and class distinctions follow—The church rent by dissension—Deeds of darkness.............. 410

Chap. 7—Chief judge murdered and government overthrown—Division into

The "Synopsis of Chapters" at the back of the 1920 edition of the Book of Mormon.

PRONOUNCING VOCABULARY

MOSTLY PROPER NAMES OF BOOK OF MORMON ORIGIN

With some Biblical names included

Aaron—ār′ŏn
Abel—ā′bel
Abinadi—a-bĭn′a-dī
Abinadom—a-bĭn′a-dŏm
Abish—ā′bĭsh
Ablom—ăb′lŏm
Abraham—ā′bra-hăm
Agosh—ā′gŏsh
Aha—ā′hä
Ahah—ā′hä
Ahaz—ā′hăz
Aiath—a-ī′ath
Akish—ā′kĭsh
Alma—ăl′mä
Amaleki—a-măl′ĕ-kī
Amalekites—a-măl′ĕ-kītes
Amalickiah—a-mă-lĭ-kī′ä
Amalickiahites—a-mă-lĭ-kī′ä-hītes
Amaron—ă-mā′rŏn
Amgid—ăm′gĭd
Aminadab—a-mĭn′a-dăb
Aminadi—a-mĭn′a-dī
Amlici—ăm′lĭ-cī
Amlicites—ăm′lĭ-cītes
Ammah—ăm′mä
Ammaron—ăm′ar-on

Ammon—ăm′ŏn
Ammonites—ăm′ŏn-ītes
Ammonihah—ăm-ŏn-ī′hä
Ammonihahites—ăm-ŏn-ī′hä-hītes
Ammoron—ăm′ōr-ŏn
Amnigaddah—ăm-nĭ-găd′dä
Amnihu—ăm-nī′hū
Amnor—ăm′nôr
Amoron—ă-mō′rŏn
Amos—ā′mŏs
Amulek—ăm′ū-lĕk
Amulon—ăm′ū-lŏn
Amulonites—ăm′ū-lŏn-ītes
Anathoth—ăn′a-thoth
Angola—ăn-gō′la
Ani-Anti—ăn′ī-ăn′tī
Anti-Nephi-Lehi—ăn′tī-nē′phī-lē′hī
Anti-Nephi-Lehies—ăn′tī-nē′phī-lē′hīes
Antiomno—ăn-tī-ŏm′nō
Antion—ăn′tī-ŏn
Antionah—ăn-tī-ōn′ä
Antionum—ăn-tī-ōn′ŭm
Antiparah—ăn-tī-pâr′ä
Antipas—ăn′tī-pas
Antipus—ăn′tī-pŭs

531

The "Pronouncing Vocabulary" from the 1920 edition.

THE BOOK OF MORMON

An Account Written by

THE HAND OF MORMON
UPON PLATES

TAKEN FROM THE PLATES OF NEPHI

Wherefore, it is an abridgment of the record of the people of Nephi, and also of the Lamanites—Written to the Lamanites, who are a remnant of the house of Israel; and also to Jew and Gentile—Written by way of commandment, and also by the spirit of prophecy and of revelation—Written and sealed up, and hid up unto the Lord, that they might not be destroyed—To come forth by the gift and power of God unto the interpretation thereof—Sealed by the hand of Moroni, and hid up unto the Lord, to come forth in due time by way of the Gentile—The interpretation thereof by the gift of God.

An abridgment taken from the Book of Ether also, which is a record of the people of Jared, who were scattered at the time the Lord confounded the language of the people, when they were building a tower to get to heaven—Which is to show unto the remnant of the House of Israel what great things the Lord hath done for their fathers; and that they may know the covenants of the Lord, that they are not cast off forever—And also to the convincing of the Jew and Gentile that JESUS is the CHRIST, the ETERNAL GOD, manifesting himself unto all nations—And now, if there are faults they are the mistakes of men; wherefore, condemn not the things of God, that ye may be found spotless at the judgment-seat of Christ.

TRANSLATED BY JOSEPH SMITH, JUN.

PUBLISHED BY
The Church of Jesus Christ of Latter-day Saints
SALT LAKE CITY, UTAH, U. S. A.
1920

The title page of the 1920 edition, which was not actually released until 1921.

Publication of the 1920 edition of the Book of Mormon took longer than expected, and its actual release date was 1921.[19] In March 1921, scriptures committee member Anthony W. Ivins was called into the First Presidency.[20] During the April 1921 general conference of the Church, he introduced the new edition of the Book of Mormon to the members of the Church, explaining its features, which he said included "a pronouncing vocabulary."

Holding the new edition in his hand, President Ivins rehearsed the work of the scriptures committee and recounted the advantages of the new volume, including "a brief synopsis of the contents of the book and the story of its origin as related by Joseph Smith." Some other features were a modern table of contents, designated "Names and Order of Books in the Book of Mormon," as well as carefully revised footnotes "and a very greatly improved index which facilitates the study of the book."

"So we have brought out a new edition of this book," President Ivins said, "which is of such great interest to the Church and its members, which we recommend to you, my brethren and sisters, and to all other people for study."

He concluded by testifying that the Book of Mormon was "the word of the Lord brought forth through the instrumentality of Joseph Smith for the redemption of mankind, to go with the Bible as an additional evidence and witness to the people of the world that the decrees of the Father are unchangeable, that the words of the prophets will be fulfilled, that Israel will be gathered, and that redemption will come to the covenant people of the Lord."

"Search the scriptures, my brethren and sisters," he urged, "for in them we have eternal life, and they are they which testify of God and of the truth of these things which I have said to you. I pray that we may all become familiar with them, that we may all, through adherence to their tenets, attain to everlasting life, through Jesus Christ."[21]

The last decades of the twentieth century saw the construction of the new Church Office Building shown here, which was completed in 1972, and new editions of the scriptures.

Chapter Nine
THE 1981 EDITION

The 1920 edition of the Book of Mormon served as the basis for all other printings over the next six decades.[1] But it could still be improved, and that improvement came, finally, as a result of an effort to publish a Latter-day Saint edition of the King James Version of the Bible.

From the Church's beginnings, its members had used Bibles printed by others. Over time, Church entities began purchasing Bibles from major publishers imprinted with the Church's name. In general, the traditional study aids in these Bibles remained unchanged, though Latter-day Saint reference aids were often bound in with them to help members in their scripture study.[2]

By the early 1970s, decades of effort to correlate all Church programs under priesthood direction had culminated in a unified curriculum focused on the scriptures. Church leaders hoped this curriculum would lead to better gospel study, resulting in more devout, dedicated Saints.[3]

As these leaders pondered how to improve gospel study, they decided for the first time to create an edition of the King James Version of the Bible that would be closely cross-referenced to the Book of Mormon and other Latter-day

Saint scriptures. This project led to the decision to create new editions of the Church's other standard works, including the Book of Mormon.[4]

Thomas S. Monson.

The Scriptures Publication Committee appointed to oversee production of these new editions was ultimately made up of three members of the Quorum of the Twelve Apostles: Thomas S. Monson, Boyd K. Packer, and Bruce R. McConkie.[5] They were assisted by key staff members and a veritable army of other helpers in what was the most labor-intensive scripture publication effort in the Church's history.[6]

Each of the apostles and the key staffers brought a lifetime of experience and important talents to the project. Elder Monson, chair of the committee, brought both administrative skills and publishing experience from his early career as a printer. He gave overall supervision to the project and made resources available to the staff and volunteers working on it.[7]

Boyd K. Packer.

Elder Packer was a teacher, and he worked to ensure that the scriptures could be used effectively by Church members in learning the doctrines of the gospel. He helped oversee development of the Topical Guide in the Bible to which the Book of Mormon notes referred.[8]

Bruce R. McConkie.

Elder McConkie was known for his gospel scholarship. He was responsible for overseeing development of the footnotes as well as the summaries that appeared at the beginning of each chapter in all four of the standard works.[9]

THE 1981 EDITION

The new Latter-day Saint edition of the Bible appeared in 1979 and the Book of Mormon and other standard works in 1981. The Book of Mormon had several improved features. It began with a new "Introduction," which described the nature of the volume, gave a brief history of its origin, made clear its significance, and invited all to read it, ponder its message, and ask God "if the book is true."[10]

The testimonies of the Three Witnesses and the Eight Witnesses were followed by a "Testimony of the Prophet Joseph Smith," which was a revised version of the section in the 1920 edition titled "Origin of the Book of Mormon."[11]

In the 1920 edition, the title and copyright pages had been followed by a page headed "Brief Analysis of the Book of Mormon." The 1981 edition put this section after Joseph Smith's testimony and retitled it "A Brief Explanation about the Book of Mormon."[12]

The summaries that headed each chapter of the 1920 edition were revised and expanded in the 1981 edition.[13] The "Synopsis of Chapters" at the end of the 1920 edition was eliminated as redundant.[14]

One of the most noticeable differences in the 1981 edition was the book's footnotes. They went from a simple, single-column format with relatively few references to a vastly expanded three-column format containing many references to the Topical Guide that appeared in the 1979 Latter-day Saint edition of the Bible. The three-column format of the notes carried over from that edition of the Bible.[15]

So did the numbering of the footnotes. In the 1920 edition, the footnotes had followed the traditional Bible system of beginning with the lowercase letter *a* and continuing through the alphabet to the end of the chapter, sometimes

THE BOOK OF MORMON

THE FIRST BOOK OF NEPHI

HIS REIGN AND MINISTRY

An account of Lehi and his wife Sariah, and his four sons, being called, (beginning at the eldest) Laman, Lemuel, Sam, and Nephi. The Lord warns Lehi to depart out of the land of Jerusalem, because he prophesieth unto the people concerning their iniquity and they seek to destroy his life. He taketh three days' journey into the wilderness with his family. Nephi taketh his brethren and returneth to the land of Jerusalem after the record of the Jews. The account of their sufferings. They take the daughters of Ishmael to wife. They take their families and depart into the wilderness. Their sufferings and afflictions in the wilderness. The course of their travels. They come to the large waters. Nephi's brethren rebel against him. He confoundeth them, and buildeth a ship. They call the place Bountiful. They cross the large waters into the promised land, &c. This is according to the account of Nephi; or in other words, I, Nephi, wrote this record.

CHAPTER 1.

Lehi's vision of the pillar of fire and the book of prophecy—He predicts the impending fate of Jerusalem, and foretells the coming of the Messiah—The Jews seek his life.

1. I, Nephi, having been born of goodly parents, therefore I was taught somewhat in all the learning of my father; and having seen many afflictions in the course of my days, nevertheless, having been highly favored of the Lord in all my days; yea, having had a great knowledge of the goodness and the mysteries of God, therefore I make a record of my proceedings in my days.

2. Yea, I make a record in the language of my father, which consists of the learning of the Jews and the *a*language of the Egyptians.

3. And I know that the record which I make is true; and I make it with mine own hand; and I make it according to my knowledge.

4. For it came to pass in the commencement of the *b*first year of the reign of Zedekiah, king of Judah, (my father, Lehi, having dwelt at Jerusalem in all his days); and in that same year there came *c*many prophets, prophesying unto the people that they must repent, or the great city Jerusalem must be destroyed.

5. Wherefore it came to pass that my father, Lehi, as he went forth prayed unto the Lord, yea,

a, Mos. 1:4. Morm. 9:32.   *b*, 2 Kings 24:17, 18.   *c*, 2 Chron. 36:15, 16.
ABOUT B. C. 600.

The 1920 edition of the Book of Mormon, showing limited chapter headnotes and footnotes.

THE FIRST BOOK OF NEPHI

HIS REIGN AND MINISTRY

An account of Lehi and his wife Sariah, and his four sons, being called, (beginning at the eldest) Laman, Lemuel, Sam, and Nephi. The Lord warns Lehi to depart out of the land of Jerusalem, because he prophesieth unto the people concerning their iniquity and they seek to destroy his life. He taketh three days' journey into the wilderness with his family. Nephi taketh his brethren and returneth to the land of Jerusalem after the record of the Jews. The account of their sufferings. They take the daughters of Ishmael to wife. They take their families and depart into the wilderness. Their sufferings and afflictions in the wilderness. The course of their travels. They come to the large waters. Nephi's brethren rebel against him. He confoundeth them, and buildeth a ship. They call the name of the place Bountiful. They cross the large waters into the promised land, and so forth. This is according to the account of Nephi; or in other words, I, Nephi, wrote this record.

CHAPTER 1

Nephi begins the record of his people—Lehi sees in vision a pillar of fire and reads from a book of prophecy—He praises God, foretells the coming of the Messiah, and prophesies the destruction of Jerusalem—He is persecuted by the Jews.

I, NEPHI, having been ^{a}born of ^{b}goodly ^{c}parents, therefore I was ^{d}taught somewhat in all the learning of my father; and having seen many ^{e}afflictions in the course of my days, nevertheless, having been highly favored of the Lord in all my days; yea, having had a great knowledge of the goodness and the mysteries of God, therefore I make a ^{f}record of my proceedings in my days.

2 Yea, I make a record in the ^{a}language of my father, which consists of the learning of the Jews and the language of the Egyptians.

3 And I know that the record which I make is ^{a}true; and I make it with mine own hand; and I make it according to my knowledge.

4 For it came to pass in the commencement of the ^{a}first year of the reign of ^{b}Zedekiah, king of Judah, (my father, Lehi, having dwelt at ^{c}Jerusalem in all his days); and in that same year there came many ^{d}prophets, prophesying unto the people that they must ^{e}repent, or the great city ^{f}Jerusalem must be destroyed.

5 Wherefore it came to pass that my father, Lehi, as he went forth prayed unto the Lord, yea, even

---

1 1a TG Birthright.
  b Prov. 22:1.
  c Mosiah 1:2 (2–3);
    D&C 68:25 (25, 28).
    TG Honoring Father
    and Mother.
  d Enos 1:1.
    TG Education;
    Family, Children,
    Responsibilities
    toward;
    Family, Love within.
  e TG Affliction; Blessing;
    God, Gifts of.
  f TG Record Keeping;
    Scriptures, Writing of.

2a Mosiah 1:4;
    Morm. 9:32 (32–33).
3a 1 Ne. 14:30;
    2 Ne. 25:20;
    Mosiah 1:6;
    Alma 3:12;
    Ether 5:3 (1–3).
4a 1 Ne. 2:4;
    Mosiah 6:4.
  b 2 Kgs. 24:18;
    2 Chr. 36:10;
    Jer. 37:1; 44:30;
    49:34; 52:3 (3–5);
    Omni 1:15.
  c 1 Chr. 9:3;

2 Chr. 15:9;
    Alma 7:10.
  d 2 Kgs. 17:13 (13–15);
    2 Chr. 36:15 (15–16);
    Jer. 7:25; 26:20.
    TG Prophets,
    Mission of.
  e TG Repentance.
  f Jer. 26:18 (17–19);
    2 Ne. 1:4;
    Hel. 8:20.
    TG Israel, Bondage of,
    in Other Lands;
    Jerusalem.

[About 600 B.C.]

The 1981 edition with improved headnotes and footnotes integrated with the other scriptures.

becoming quite complicated. The new, simplified system started over with each verse, an innovation that was easy to follow.[16]

There were also changes in the text of the Book of Mormon itself. The Church now had improved access to the surviving pages of the original and printer's manuscripts of the Book of Mormon. The original had remained in the Nauvoo House cornerstone until 1882, when Emma Smith's second husband removed it and gave portions away. Many surviving pages of the manuscript did not come into Church possession again until after the 1920 edition had been published.[17]

The printer's manuscript was retained by Oliver Cowdery until he died, when it went to his brother-in-law and fellow Book of Mormon witness David Whitmer. One of David's grandsons sold it to the Reorganized Church of Jesus Christ of Latter Day Saints in 1903.[18] By the mid-1970s, excellent relations between scholars in the Church Historical Department and the historical staff of the Reorganized Church resulted in exchanging copies of important documents, including the printer's manuscript.[19]

A study of these documents and earlier editions of the Book of Mormon led to textual corrections.[20] One of the most notable was restoring the change Joseph Smith made to 2 Nephi in the 1840 edition, replacing "a white and a delightsome people" with "a pure and a delightsome people."[21] Because later Latter-day Saint editions of the Book of Mormon descended from the 1841 Liverpool edition, which followed the text of the 1837 edition, they lacked Joseph Smith's correction until it was restored in the 1981 edition.[22]

Most other changes to the text were minor.[23] As a result of the textual improvements made in the 1981 edition, it bore a note that read: "About this edition: Some minor errors in the text have been perpetuated in past editions of the Book of Mormon. This edition contains corrections that seem appropriate to bring the material into conformity with prepublication manuscripts and early editions edited by the Prophet Joseph Smith."[24]

An Old Testament prophecy refers to "the stick of Joseph" and "the stick of Judah" which, the Lord says, "shall be one in mine hand."[25] In the 1979 Latter-day Saint edition of the Bible, the chapter summary for this prophecy explains, "The stick of Judah (Bible) and the stick of Joseph (Book of Mormon) become one in the Lord's hand."[26]

With the completion of the 1981 edition of the Book of Mormon as a companion to the 1979 Latter-day Saint edition of the Bible, the new Bible and triple combination (Book of Mormon, Doctrine and Covenants, and Pearl of Great Price) fit together internally, not just because they were bound in similar materials.[27]

The closeness of these scriptures gave rise to a popular new form of the standard works: the integrated quadruple combination, or "quad," as it is popularly known. Now these four books of scripture could be "one in the . . . hand" in a way they had never been before.[28]

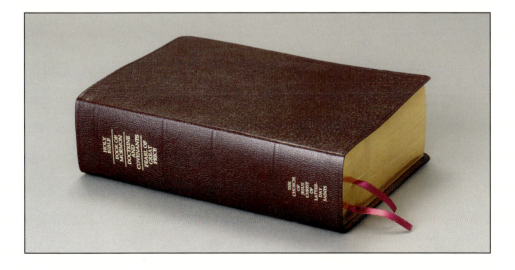

The new quadruple combination made the Bible and Book of Mormon "one in the . . . hand."

Yet one thing more was needed to improve the 1981 edition of the Book of Mormon. The Topical Guide and chapter headings in the 1979 Latter-day Saint edition of the Bible demonstrated dramatically how frequently the Old Testament, the New Testament, and the Book of Mormon pointed to the Lord Jesus Christ.

Elder Boyd K. Packer, who oversaw production of the Topical Guide, later explained:

> The subject "Jesus Christ" in the topical guide takes eighteen pages of small print just to list the references. It is the most comprehensive compilation of scriptural information on the mission and teachings of the Lord Jesus Christ that has ever been assembled in the history of the world.[29]

The Old Testament testified of Jesus Christ in His premortal state and prophesied of His coming. The New Testament testified of the mortal life, ministry, and resurrection of the Savior, prophesying also of His Second Coming. Because the Book of Mormon did all these things and recounted the Lord's covenant with another ancient people, it too could properly be called a "testament." In the 1982 printing of the 1981 edition, a subtitle was added to the Book of Mormon. It would now be known as "Another Testament of Jesus Christ."[30]

Elder Packer said, "With the passing of years, these scriptures will produce successive generations of faithful Christians who know the Lord Jesus Christ and are disposed to obey His will. . . . The revelations will be opened to them as to no other in the history of the world. Into their hands now are placed the sticks of Joseph and of Judah. They will develop a gospel scholarship beyond that which their forebears could achieve. They will have the testimony that Jesus is the Christ and be competent to proclaim Him and to defend Him."[31]

THE
HOLY BIBLE

CONTAINING THE

OLD AND NEW TESTAMENTS

TRANSLATED OUT OF THE
ORIGINAL TONGUES: AND WITH THE
FORMER TRANSLATIONS DILIGENTLY COMPARED
AND REVISED, BY HIS MAJESTY'S
SPECIAL COMMAND

AUTHORIZED KING JAMES VERSION
WITH EXPLANATORY NOTES AND
CROSS REFERENCES TO THE STANDARD WORKS
OF THE CHURCH OF JESUS CHRIST
OF LATTER-DAY SAINTS

PUBLISHED BY
THE CHURCH OF JESUS CHRIST
OF LATTER-DAY SAINTS
SALT LAKE CITY, UTAH, U.S.A.
1979

Title page of the 1979 Latter-day Saint edition of the Bible, complete with a topical guide that references the Book of Mormon and other scriptures testifying of the Lord Jesus Christ.

The Conference Center (dedicated 2000) in downtown Salt Lake City heralds the continuing unfolding of the Church around the world.

Chapter Ten
"The Keystone of Our Religion"

From the first edition in 1830 to the latest edition more than a century and a half later, the Book of Mormon has become increasingly easier to read and understand:

- The 1830 edition made the Book of Mormon record available in book form to the world for the first time.[1]
- The 1837 edition corrected the printed text against the printer's manuscript, helped standardize the English, and offered a more portable format.[2]
- The 1840 edition included corrections made by Joseph Smith, who discovered errors as he proofread the printed text against the original manuscript.[3]
- The 1841 first European edition made the book more widely available in England and became the textual basis for subsequent editions.[4]
- The 1852 edition provided numbered paragraphs.
- The 1879 edition broke down the large chapters and verses into sizes that were much easier for gospel study and instruction.[5]
- The 1920 edition standardized chapter titles, further modernized the

grammar, provided useful chapter summaries, and presented the text in double-column format like many modern Bibles.[6]

- The 1981 edition improved the text based on enhanced access to early manuscripts and editions and fully integrated the book with the Bible and the Church's other scriptures, providing study helps that point readers more than ever to Jesus Christ.[7]
- In 1982, the subtitle "Another Testament of Jesus Christ" was added to emphasize the book's role in bringing readers to Christ.[8]

On November 28, 1841, Joseph Smith declared to a group of Church leaders in Nauvoo "that the Book of Mormon was the most correct of any book on earth, and the keystone of our religion, and a man would get nearer to God by abiding by its precepts, than by any other book."[9] The improvements made in the book's editions over the years have provided readers today with the most correct version of the most correct book on earth.[10]

Still, the Book of Mormon does not claim to be perfect. "If there are faults," Moroni wrote on the title page, "they are the mistakes of men; wherefore, condemn not the things of God."[11] But the book does claim to lead readers to Christ, in whom *they* can be made perfect.[12]

Every official edition of the Book of Mormon has included the testimony of eleven witnesses—all contemporaries of Joseph Smith—who saw the golden plates from which the Book of Mormon was translated. In early editions, the witnesses' statements were in the back of the book. Today, they are in the front.[13]

Eight men bore witness that Joseph Smith showed the plates to them and that the record had "the appearance of gold." The witnesses further testified, "And as many of the leaves as the said Smith has translated we did handle with our hands; and we also saw the engravings thereon, all of which has the appearance of

Wilford Woodruff.

Wilford Woodruff's journal records Joseph Smith's statement about the Book of Mormon.

THE TESTIMONY OF THREE WITNESSES.

Be it known unto all nations, kindreds, tongues, and people, unto whom this work shall come, that we, through the grace of God the Father, and our Lord Jesus Christ, have seen the plates which contain this record, which is a record of the people of Nephi, and also of the Lamanites, his brethren, and also of the people of Jared, which came from the tower of which hath been spoken; and we also know that they have been translated by the gift and power of God, for his voice hath declared it unto us; wherefore we know of a surety, that the work is true. And we also testify that we have seen the engravings which are upon the plates; and they have been shewn unto us by the power of God, and not of man. And we declare with words of soberness, that an Angel of God came down from heaven, and he brought and laid before our eyes, that we beheld and saw the plates, and the engravings thereon; and we know that it is by the grace of God the Father, and our Lord Jesus Christ, that we beheld and bear record that these things are true; and it is marvellous in our eyes: Nevertheless, the voice of the Lord commanded us that we should bear record of it; wherefore, to be obedient unto the commandments of God, we bear testimony of these things.— And we know that if we are faithful in Christ, we shall rid our garments of the blood of all men, and be found spotless before the judgement seat of Christ, and shall dwell with him eternally in the heavens. And the honor be to the Father, and to the Son, and to the Holy Ghost, which is one God. Amen.

OLIVER COWDERY,
DAVID WHITMER,
MARTIN HARRIS.

The testimony of the Three Witnesses from the first edition of the Book of Mormon (1830).

ancient work, and of curious workmanship. And this we bear record with words of soberness, that the said Smith has shown unto us, for we have seen and hefted, and know of a surety that the said Smith has got the plates of which we have spoken. And we give our names unto the world, to witness unto the world that which we have seen. And we lie not, God bearing witness of it."[14]

Oliver Cowdery, David Whitmer, and Martin Harris solemnly testified that they had "seen the plates," which were shown them by an angel. "And we also know that they have been translated by the gift and power of God," they attested, "for his voice hath declared it unto us; wherefore we know of a surety that the work is true." That same voice "commanded us that we should bear record of it; wherefore, to be obedient unto the commandments of God, we bear testimony of these things. And we know that if we are faithful in Christ, we shall rid our garments of the blood of all men, and be found spotless before the judgment-seat of Christ, and shall dwell with him eternally in the heavens."[15]

In the end, Joseph Smith and his elder brother Hyrum gave their lives as a testimony. In mid-1844, opposition to the Latter-day Saints caused the two men to flee their homes in Nauvoo, Illinois, and cross the Mississippi River to the west. Their flight was a precursor to the great western trek of the Saints led years later by Brigham Young.[16]

Because their opponents had focused attention principally on them, Joseph and Hyrum left, believing that their flight would protect the Saints who remained in Nauvoo. Some of their followers, however, called their escape cowardice—leaving the people when they needed them most.

Stung by the accusations, Joseph returned to Nauvoo with Hyrum, exclaiming, "If my life is of no value to my friends, it is of no value to me."[17]

Electing to face their accusers, on the morning of June 24 Joseph and

Hyrum left for Carthage, Illinois, the county seat. There they were thrown into jail, charged with treason because Joseph had called out the city's state-sanctioned militia to defend the people against threats of violence.[18]

Knowing his enemies intended to kill him, Joseph said as he went to Carthage, "I am going like a lamb to the slaughter; but I am calm as a summer's morning; I have a conscience void of offense towards God, and towards all men. I SHALL DIE INNOCENT, AND IT SHALL YET BE SAID OF ME—HE WAS MURDERED IN COLD BLOOD."[19]

The morning they left for Carthage, Hyrum felt troubled and went to the Book of Mormon for comfort. He and Joseph were about to turn themselves over to "gentiles"—people not of their faith. Hyrum hoped they would have compassion on the Church leaders, in spite of the mob spirit that raged in the region.

Hyrum opened the book to a passage that had great meaning to him. Under the circumstances, it became a prayer. The verse began: "And it came to pass that I prayed unto the Lord that he would give unto the Gentiles grace, that they might have charity."[20]

But they did not have charity. On June 27, 1844, a little after 5:00 P.M., a mob of between 150 and 200 men stormed the jail and shot Joseph and Hyrum multiple times, brutally killing both.[21]

John Taylor, a friend and fellow Church leader, was in the jail at the time and sustained severe gunshot wounds himself. After returning to Nauvoo, he returned also to a printing project he had nearly finished before leaving with Joseph and Hyrum for Carthage. It was the second edition of the Doctrine and Covenants, a book containing revelations of Joseph Smith. Before binding the printed pages into book form, John Taylor added a tribute to the murdered leaders.

610   BOOK OF ETHER.

now I know that this love which thou hast had for the children of men, is charity; wherefore, except men shall have charity, they cannot inherit that place which thou hast prepared in the mansions of thy father. Wherefore, I know by this thing which thou hast said, that if the Gentiles have not charity, because of our weakness, that thou wilt prove them, and take away their talent, yea, even that which they have received, and give unto them who shall have more abundantly.

And it came to pass that I prayed unto the Lord that he would give unto the Gentiles grace, that they might have charity. And it came to pass that the Lord said unto me, if they have not charity, it mattereth not unto thee, thou hast been faithful; whrefore thy garments shall be made clean. And because thou hast seen thy weakness, thou shalt be made strong, even unto the sitting down in the place which I have prepared in the mansions of my Father. And now I, Moroni, bid farewell unto the Gentiles, yea, and also unto my brethren whom I love, until we shall meet before the judgment seat of Christ, where all men shall know that my garments are not spotted with your blood, and then shall ye know that I have seen Jesus, and that he hath talked with me face to face, and that he told me in plain humility, even as a man telleth another in mine own language, concerning these things; and only a few have I written, because of my weakness in writing. And now I would commend you to seek this Jesus of whom the prophets and apostles have written, that the grace of God the Father, and also the Lord Jesus Christ, and the Holy Ghost, which beareth record of them, may be, and abide in you for ever. Amen.

CHAPTER VI.

And now I, Moroni, proceed to finish my record concerning the destruction of the people of whom I have been writing. For behold, they rejected all the words of Ether; for he truly told them of all things, from the beginning of man; and that after the waters had receded from off the face of this land, it became a choice land above all other lands, a chosen land of the Lord; wherefore the Lord would have that all men should serve him,

Hyrum Smith's copy of the 1841 edition of the Book of Mormon. He read and turned down this page before leaving for Carthage, where he was murdered.

Joseph Smith (right) and his brother Hyrum.

Martyrdom of Joseph Smith.

"Henceforward," he wrote, "their names will be classed among the martyrs of religion; and the reader in every nation will be reminded that the Book of Mormon, and this book of Doctrine and Covenants of the church, cost the best blood of the nineteenth century to bring them forth for the salvation of a ruined world."[22]

Like the Book of Mormon itself, the introduction to the 1981 edition includes a challenge and a promise to everyone throughout the world:

> We invite all men everywhere to read the Book of Mormon, to ponder in their hearts the message it contains, and then to ask God, the Eternal Father, in the name of Christ if the book is true. Those who pursue this course and ask in faith will gain a testimony of its truth and divinity by the power of the Holy Ghost. (See Moroni 10:3–5.)
>
> Those who gain this divine witness from the Holy Spirit will also come to know by the same power that Jesus Christ is the Savior

of the world, that Joseph Smith is his revelator and prophet in these last days, and that The Church of Jesus Christ of Latter-day Saints is the Lord's kingdom once again established on the earth, preparatory to the second coming of the Messiah.[23]

Today, millions of Latter-day Saints, speaking more than 150 languages around the world, stand as witnesses that the book is true and invite all mankind to "come unto Christ" and enjoy the peace and happiness that follow.[24]

In so doing, they echo the words of the prophet-historian Moroni, who preserved the Book of Mormon plates, delivered them temporarily to Joseph Smith, and received them back from him.[25] Moroni invited all to come unto Christ and be sanctified through His Atonement. Moroni promised that they would see him someday and be accountable for whether they had accepted his challenge. At the end of the Book of Mormon, he wrote:

> Remember these things; for the time speedily cometh that ye shall know that I lie not, for ye shall see me at the bar of God; and the Lord God will say unto you: Did I not declare my words unto you, which were written by this man, like as one crying from the dead, yea, even as one speaking out of the dust? . . .
>
> And God shall show unto you, that that which I have written is true. . . .
>
> And now I bid unto all, farewell. I soon go to rest in the paradise of God, until my spirit and body shall again reunite, and I am brought forth triumphant through the air, to meet you before the pleasing bar of the great Jehovah, the Eternal Judge of both quick and dead. Amen.[26]

Sculpture of the angel Moroni atop the Salt Lake Temple.

Notes

Books in the Book of Mormon

1 Nephi	Jarom	Alma	Mormon
2 Nephi	Omni	Helaman	Ether
Jacob	Words of Mormon	3 Nephi	Moroni
Enos	Mosiah	4 Nephi	

Abbreviations

D&C: The Doctrine and Covenants of The Church of Jesus Christ of Latter-day Saints (Salt Lake City, UT: The Church of Jesus Christ of Latter-day Saints, 1981)

JS–H: Joseph Smith–History, in The Pearl of Great Price (Salt Lake City, UT: The Church of Jesus Christ of Latter-day Saints, 1981)

Preface

1. "Book of Mormon: 150 million copies," *Church News,* April 22, 2011; Ryan Kunz, "180 Years Later, Book of Mormon Nears 150 Million Copies," *Ensign,* March 2010, 74–76. This book has been published in full in 82 languages and partially in 25 more.

2. *Biographia Literaria* (London: William Clowes and Sons, 1817), 145.

3. Alma 32:27.

Prologue

1. Helaman 2:13–14; 6:17–29; 3 Nephi 3:9; 4:5; 4 Nephi 1:35–48. The dates we use in this chapter follow those that appear in the current edition of the Book of Mormon. On when dates were added to the Book of Mormon, see Royal Skousen, "Book of Mormon, editions of," in Dennis L. Largey, gen. ed., *Book of Mormon Reference Companion* (Salt Lake City, UT: Deseret Book, 2003), 113. On the

accuracy of these dates, see Jeffrey R. Chadwick, "Dating the Birth of Jesus Christ," *BYU Studies* 49, no. 4 (2010): 4–38.

2. Enos 1:14–16; Omni 1:14–17; Mosiah 1:2–5; Alma 14: 8, 14; Alma 23:5; Alma 37:1, 3, 9; Alma 46:13–16; 4 Nephi 1:46–48; Mormon 6:6.

3. 4 Nephi 1:48–49.

4. Mosiah 18; 25:18; 26:15; Alma 5:3; Mormon 1:2, 5.

5. Mormon 1:2–3.

6. Mormon 1:3–5.

7. Mormon 1:6–12.

8. Mormon 1:13–15.

9. Mormon 1:16–19.

10. 1 Nephi 4:31; Mormon 2:1–2.

11. Mormon 2:8–12.

12. Mormon 2:13–14.

13. Mormon 1:3–4; 2:17–18.

14. Mormon 2:19–6:5.

15. Mormon 6:6. See also Words of Mormon 1:1–2.

16. Alma 43–63; Byron R. Merrill, "Moroni," in Largey, *Book of Mormon Reference Companion,* 557.

17. Mormon 6:7–15. In addition to Mormon and those who survived with him, verse 15 says there were "also a few who had escaped into the south countries, and a few who had deserted over unto the Lamanites."

18. Mormon 8:2–3, 6–7.

19. Mormon 8–9; Moroni 1–10.

20. Mormon 9:34; Ether 3:22–24, 28; 4:4–7; D&C 17:1. JS–H 1:35, 42, 52, 59, 62, and D&C 17:1 designate these interpreters as "Urim and Thummim," relating them to instruments used in the Old Testament. See Exodus 28:30; Leviticus 8:8; Deuteronomy 33:8; Ezra 2:63; Nehemiah 7:65.

21. Mormon 8:16, 22.

Chapter One: The Golden Plates

1. JS–H 1:3, 27–51; Lucy [Mack] Smith, *Biographical Sketches of Joseph Smith, the Prophet, and His Progenitors for Many Generations* (Liverpool: S. W. Richards, 1853), 78–82.

2. JS–H 1:35, 51–52.

3. JS–H 1:46, 53; Oliver Cowdery to W. W. Phelps, "Letter VIII," *Messenger and Advocate* 2 (October 1835): 197–98; Lucy [Mack] Smith, *Biographical Sketches,* 70–72.

4. JS–H 1:53; Cowdery to Phelps, "Letter VIII," 197–98. Joseph Smith led the committee that produced the first edition of the Doctrine and Covenants, a book of Latter-day Saint scripture, in 1835. One passage in the book mentions "Moroni, whom I have sent unto you to reveal the Book of Mormon." Doctrine and Covenants of the Church of the Latter Day Saints (Kirtland, OH: F. G. Williams & Co., 1835), 180, current D&C 27:5. In one of the first published histories of the Book of Mormon, Joseph's close

associate Oliver Cowdery also referred to "the angel Moroni, . . . who communicated the knowledge of the record of the Nephites, in this age" and who "hid up" the record "unto the Lord." Oliver Cowdery to W. W. Phelps, "Letter VI," in *Messenger and Advocate* 1 (April 1835): 112. In 1838, in answer to the question "How, and where did you obtain the book of Mormon?" Joseph replied, "Moroni, the person who deposited the plates . . . appeared unto me, and told me where they were." *Elders' Journal* 1 (July 1838): 42–43. Joseph Smith's 1839 history, penned by clerks, used the name "Nephi" instead of "Moroni," a mistake that tracked into later publications before being corrected. Dean C. Jessee, ed., *The Papers of Joseph Smith,* vol. 1 (Salt Lake City, UT: Deseret Book, 1989), 277.

5. JS–H 1:59; Lucy [Mack] Smith, *Biographical Sketches,* 92–93, 98–101.

6. JS–H 1:60; Alexander L. Baugh, "Gold plates," in Dennis L. Largey, gen. ed., *Book of Mormon Reference Companion* (Salt Lake City, UT: Deseret Book, 2003), 299–300.

7. Joseph Smith to John Wentworth, in Jessee, *Papers of Joseph Smith,* 431. Baugh, "Gold plates," notes the varying dimensions given much later by Martin Harris and David Whitmer but considers Joseph's description "the most accurate and reliable." Joseph's dimensions, given in 1842, seem borne out by the earliest published dimensions of the volume, "8 inches long, 6 wide." *Palmyra Freeman,* as cited in "Golden Bible," *Rochester Advertiser and Daily Telegraph* (New York), August 31, 1829. Joseph's description of the plates as having the "appearance of gold" has led some scholars to conclude that they were a gold alloy, perhaps "gold mixed with copper and silver to make approximately 8-carat gold material." Baugh, "Gold plates," citing Reed H. Putnam, "Were the Golden Plates Made of Tumbaga?" *Improvement Era,* September 1966, 788–89, 828–30.

8. Smith to Wentworth, in Jessee, *Papers of Joseph Smith,* 431.

9. See Baugh, "Gold plates." In 1856, Orson Pratt, a close friend and contemporary of Joseph (though not an eyewitness of the plates), also said two-thirds of the plates were sealed. Alexander L. Baugh, "Sealed portion of the gold plates," in Largey, *Book of Mormon Reference Companion,* 707. On the characterization of Martin, see JS–H 1:61.

10. Emma Hale Smith Bidamon, "Last Testimony of Sister Emma," *Saints' Herald* 26 (October 1, 1879), 290, cited in Baugh, "Gold plates," 299.

11. 1 Nephi 1:2; Mosiah 1:4; Mormon 9:32–33; Dallin D. Oaks, "Book of Mormon, language of the translated text of," in Largey, *Book of Mormon Reference Companion,* 116–19; Donald W. Parry, "Hebrew language," in Largey, *Book of Mormon Reference Companion,* 325–26; Michael D. Rhodes, "Reformed Egyptian," in

Largey, *Book of Mormon Reference Companion,* 675.

12. Jessee, *Papers of Joseph Smith,* 241, 300.

13. Joseph studied Hebrew in Kirtland, Ohio, in 1835 and 1836, part of that time under the direction of instructor Joshua Seixas. Dean C. Jessee, Mark Ashurst-McGee, and Richard L. Jensen, vol. eds., *Journals, Volume 1: 1832–1839,* vol. 1 of the Journals series of *The Joseph Smith Papers,* edited by Dean C. Jessee, Ronald K. Esplin, and Richard Lyman Bushman (Salt Lake City, UT: Church Historian's Press, 2008), 107, 109, 111, 115, 116, 117, 122, 137, 140, 180, 183, 184, 186, 187, 188, 190, 191, 195, 197; Jessee, *Papers of Joseph Smith,* 104, 144–45, 152, 178, 185–87, 193.

14. 1 Nephi 9:1–6; 3 Nephi 5:8–20; Mormon 1:1–11; David Rolph Seely, "Plates of Mormon," in Largey, *Book of Mormon Reference Companion,* 644–45; David Rolph Seely, "Plates of Nephi," in Largey, *Book of Mormon Reference Companion,* 645–47.

15. Words of Mormon 1:1–2; Mormon 8–9; Ether; Moroni; *Elders' Journal* 1 (July 1838): 42–43.

16. The Book of Mormon does not mention the brother of Jared's name. But the people of the book typically named their settlements after their leaders, and Ether 2:13 calls the first major Jaredite settlement Moriancumer. In 1834, Reynolds Cahoon asked Joseph Smith to bless his newborn son. Joseph named the baby Mahonri Moriancumer and explained that was the name of the brother of Jared. "The Jaredites," *Juvenile Instructor* 27, no. 9 (1892): 282. In 1835, a publication edited by Oliver Cowdery inserted the name "Moriancumer" in brackets after "the brother of Jared." Oliver Cowdery to W. W. Phelps, "Letter VI," in *Messenger and Advocate* 1 (April 1835): 112.

17. Mosiah 28:11–20; Alma 37:21–27.

18. Ether 3:1–16.

19. Ether 3:25.

20. 2 Nephi 27:7.

21. Ether 3:21, 27; 4:1–2.

22. Ether 3:23–24, 27–28.

23. 3 Nephi 8.

24. On the passage of time, see 3 Nephi 8:5 and 3 Nephi 10:18–19. On the appearance in Bountiful, see 3 Nephi 11. On the survivors' need for repentance, see 3 Nephi 9:13.

25. Ether 4:1–2.

26. Ether 4:3–5.

27. D&C 17:1. Because Joseph had the stones, he might be tempted to read the sealed plates. But in Ether 5:1, Moroni warned him to "touch them not in order that ye may translate; for that thing is forbidden you, except by and by it shall be wisdom in God." On the future of the sealed portion, see 1 Nephi 14:26; 2 Nephi 27:7–10; Ether 4:6–7.

28. Joseph Smith Jr., [trans.], The Book of Mormon (Palmyra, NY: E. B. Grandin, 1830), [i].

29. Words of Mormon 1:8.

30. Ether 12:38–41.

31. Moroni 10:32–33.

32. Book of Mormon (1830), [i].

33. Boyd K. Packer, "Scriptures," *Ensign,* November 1982, 51; Dallin H. Oaks, "Another Testament of Jesus Christ," *Ensign,* March 1994, 60; Gaye Strathearn, "Book of Mormon: Another Testament of Jesus Christ," in Largey, *Book of Mormon Reference Companion,* 100–105.

Chapter Two: The Translation

1. Dean C. Jessee, ed., *The Papers of Joseph Smith,* vol. 1 (Salt Lake City, UT: Deseret Book, 1989), 9, 283–84; Lucy [Mack] Smith, *Biographical Sketches of Joseph Smith, the Prophet, and His Progenitors for Many Generations* (Liverpool: S. W. Richards, 1853), 112–13; JS–H 1:61.

2. JS–H 1:62–65; B. H. Roberts, *A Comprehensive History of The Church of Jesus Christ of Latter-day Saints,* 6 vols. (Provo, UT: Brigham Young University Press, 1965), 1:99–109. Joseph said that because of Martin's faith and aid to the Smiths, the Lord appeared to Martin in a vision before he took the characters to New York. Joseph also said Professor Charles Anthon's comment about not being able to read a sealed book fulfilled the prophecy in Isaiah 29:11. Jessee, *Papers of Joseph Smith,* 9, 285–86, 401.

3. Royal Skousen, *The Original Manuscript of the Book of Mormon* (Provo, UT: Foundation for Ancient Research and Mormon Studies, Brigham Young University, 2001), 3–4; Roberts, *Comprehensive History,* 1:127–33; David Whitmer, *An Address to All Believers in Christ* (Richmond, MO: n.p., 1887), 12. On the use of the seer stone interpreters, see Mosiah 28:13–16; JS–H 1:35; Richard E. Turley Jr., "Seer Stones," in Daniel H. Ludlow, ed., *Encyclopedia of Mormonism,* 4 vols. (New York: Macmillan, 1992), 3:1293.

4. General Conference Minutes, October 25, 1831, in Donald Q. Cannon and Lyndon W. Cook, *Far West Record: Minutes of The Church of Jesus Christ of Latter-day Saints, 1830–1844* (Salt Lake City, UT: Deseret Book, 1983), 23.

5. Joseph Smith Jr., [trans.], The Book of Mormon (Palmyra, NY: E. B. Grandin, 1830), [iii]. For other references to "the gift and power of God," see Omni 1:20; D&C 135:3.

6. See headnote to chapter VI, A Book of Commandments (Zion [Independence, MO]: W. W. Phelps & Co., 1833), 18, and headnote to section XXXIII of the Doctrine and Covenants of the Church of the Latter Day Saints (Kirtland, OH: F. G. Williams & Co., 1835), 160–61, current D&C 7.

7. Jessee, *Papers of Joseph Smith,* 9, 286; Skousen, *Original Manuscript,* 5.

8. Jessee, *Papers of Joseph Smith,* 9, 286.

9. Lucy [Mack] Smith, *Biographical Sketches,* 118. The date of the child's birth and death is established by his headstone in the McKune Cemetery, Susquehanna County, Pennsylvania.

10. Lucy [Mack] Smith, *Biographical Sketches,* 118.

11. Lucy [Mack] Smith, *Biographical Sketches,* 118–19.

12. Lucy [Mack] Smith, *Biographical Sketches,* 119–20.

13. Lucy [Mack] Smith, *Biographical Sketches,* 120.

14. Lucy [Mack] Smith, *Biographical Sketches,* 120–21.

15. Lucy [Mack] Smith, *Biographical Sketches,* 121–22.

16. Lucy [Mack] Smith, *Biographical Sketches,* 122–24; D&C 19.

17. Jessee, *Papers of Joseph Smith,* 10, 286–88; D&C 3, 10; Lucy [Mack] Smith, *Biographical Sketches,* 124–26, 131.

18. Jessee, *Papers of Joseph Smith,* 288; Lucy [Mack] Smith, *Biographical Sketches,* 128–31.

19. Jessee, *Papers of Joseph Smith,* 288–93; Oliver Cowdery to W. W. Phelps, September 7, 1834, in *Messenger and Advocate* 1 (October 1834): 14; John W. Welch and Tim Rathbone, "Book of Mormon Translation by Joseph Smith," in Ludlow, *Encyclopedia of Mormonism,* 1:210–13; Andrew Jenson, *Latter-day Saint Biographical Encyclopedia,* vol. 1 (Salt Lake City, UT: Andrew Jenson History Co., 1901), 249; Joseph Smith and Isaac Hale, Agreement, April 6, 1829, Joseph Smith Collection, Church History Library, Salt Lake City, Utah.

20. Skousen, *Original Manuscript,* 34–36; Milton V. Backman, "Book of Mormon, translation of," in Dennis L. Largey, gen. ed., *Book of Mormon Reference Companion* (Salt Lake City, UT: Deseret Book, 2003), 160; Neal A. Maxwell, "'By the Gift and Power of God,'" *Ensign,* January 1997, 39.

21. Cowdery to Phelps, September 7, 1834, 14.

22. Welch and Rathbone, "Book of Mormon Translation by Joseph Smith," 212; Backman, "Book of Mormon, translation of," 159–60. On the portion Joseph retained, see D&C 10:41.

23. Words of Mormon 1:3–7.

24. Welch and Rathbone, "Book of Mormon Translation by Joseph Smith," 211.

25. Jessee, *Papers of Joseph Smith,* 293; Lucy [Mack] Smith, *Biographical Sketches,* 135–37; "Report of Elders Orson Pratt and Joseph F. Smith," September 18, 1878, in *Deseret News,* November 27, 1878.

26. "Report of Elders Orson Pratt and Joseph F. Smith"; "The Eight Witnesses," *The Historical Record* 7 (October 1888): 621; Jenson, *Latter-day Saint Biographical Encyclopedia,* 1:283.

27. Jessee, *Papers of Joseph Smith,* 235–36, 294–95; 2 Nephi 11:3; 27:12–14; Ether 5:2–4; D&C 5:11–15; 17:1–9.

28. "The Testimony of Three Witnesses," Book of Mormon (1830), 589; Lucy [Mack] Smith, *Biographical Sketches,* 138–40.

29. "And Also the Testimony of Eight Witnesses," Book of Mormon (1830), 590; Lucy [Mack] Smith, *Biographical Sketches,* 140–41.

30. Lucy [Mack] Smith, *Biographical Sketches,* 139, 141; JS–H 1:59.

Chapter Three: The First Edition, 1830

1. U.S. District Court for the Northern District of New York, Copyright, June 11, 1829, Church History Library, Salt Lake City, Utah; Joseph Smith Jr., [trans.], The Book of Mormon (Palmyra, NY: E. B. Grandin, 1830), [ii]; Nathaniel Hinckley Wadsworth, "Copyright Laws and the 1830 Book of Mormon," *BYU Studies* 45, no. 3 (2006): 77, 97–99.

2. Larry C. Porter, "Grandin, Egbert Bratt," in Dennis L. Largey, gen. ed., *Book of Mormon Reference Companion* (Salt Lake City, UT: Deseret Book, 2003), 307–9; Peter Crawley, *A Descriptive Bibliography of the Mormon Church, Volume One, 1830–1847* (Provo, UT: Religious Studies Center, Brigham Young University, 1997), 29–30; John H. Gilbert, *Recollections,* September 8, 1892, typescript, Harold B. Lee Library, Brigham Young University, Provo, Utah; John H. Gilbert, *Recollections,* in Mark L. McConkie, *Remembering Joseph* (Salt Lake City, UT: Deseret Book, 2003), 235.

3. Porter, "Grandin, Egbert Bratt," in Largey, *Book of Mormon Reference Companion,* 309; Crawley, *Descriptive Bibliography,* 1:29–30; Lucy [Mack] Smith, *Biographical Sketches of Joseph Smith, the Prophet, and His Progenitors for Many Generations* (Liverpool: S. W. Richards, 1853), 142–43; Gilbert, *Recollections.*

4. Porter, "Grandin, Egbert Bratt," in Largey, *Book of Mormon Reference Companion,* 309; Crawley, *Descriptive Bibliography,* 1:29. The Rochester publisher who first agreed to print the book was Elihu F. Marshall.

5. Dean C. Jessee, ed., *The Papers of Joseph Smith,* vol. 1 (Salt Lake City: Deseret Book, 1989), 241, 300; Lucy [Mack] Smith, *Biographical Sketches,* 141–42; Gilbert, *Recollections;* Crawley, *Descriptive Bibliography,* 1:29; Larry C. Porter, "Book of Mormon, printing and publication of," in Largey, *Book of Mormon Reference Companion,* 134–35.

6. Lucy [Mack] Smith, *Biographical Sketches,* 142–43.

7. Royal Skousen, *The Printer's Manuscript of the Book of Mormon, Part One* (Provo, UT: The Foundation for Ancient Research and Mormon Studies, Brigham Young University, 2001), 3–4; Royal Skousen, "Book of Mormon, manuscripts of," in Largey, *Book of Mormon Reference Companion,* 126.

8. Porter, "Book of Mormon, printing and publication of," in Largey, *Book of Mormon Reference Companion,* 134–36.

9. Gilbert, *Recollections.* Over time, Gilbert recalled, Hyrum began bringing twice as many pages, which "would last for several days." He came to trust Gilbert enough to let him take pages home at night to punctuate so printing would go faster the next day. "The Book of Mormon," *The American Bookseller* 4 (December 15, 1877): 618. Gilbert had owned the *Wayne Sentinel* newspaper but sold it to Grandin, "after which he worked for Grandin as a compositor." Crawley, *Descriptive Bibliography,* 1:379.

10. Gilbert, *Recollections;* "He Printed the Book of Mormon," *New York Times,* June 18, 1893; Porter, "Book of Mormon, printing and publication of," in Largey, *Book of Mormon Reference Companion,* 137.

11. *The Reflector,* December 9, 22, 1829; January 2, 13, 22, 1830; Lucy [Mack] Smith, *Biographical Sketches,* 148–50; Wadsworth, "Copyright Laws and the 1830 Book of Mormon," 78–91; Andrew H. Hedges, "The Refractory Abner Cole," in Donald W. Parry, Daniel C. Peterson, and Stephen D. Ricks, eds., *Revelation, Reason, and Faith: Essays in Honor of Truman G. Madsen* (Provo, UT: Foundation for Ancient Research and Mormon Studies, Brigham Young University, 2002), 447–75. Before stopping his piracy, Cole published what is currently 1 Nephi 1:1–2:3, 1 Nephi 2:4–15, and Alma 43:22–40. Crawley, *Descriptive Bibliography,* 1:30.

12. Luther Howard to O. Dogberry, March 11, 1830, in *The Reflector,* March 16, 1830.

13. "The Book of Mormon," *Wayne Sentinel,* March 26, 1830.

14. D&C 19:26; Porter, "Book of Mormon, printing and publication of," in Largey, *Book of Mormon Reference Companion,* 138; Crawley, *Descriptive Bibliography,* 1:31.

15. Porter, "Book of Mormon, printing and publication of," in Largey, *Book of Mormon Reference Companion,* 138.

Chapter Four: The Second Edition, 1837

1. Dean C. Jessee, ed., *The Papers of Joseph Smith,* vol. 1 (Salt Lake City: Deseret Book, 1989), 241–42, 302–4; Robin Scott Jensen, Robert J. Woodford, and Steven C. Harper, vol. eds., *Manuscript Revelation Books,* facsimile edition, first (unnumbered) volume of the Revelations and Translations series of *The Joseph Smith Papers,* edited by Dean C. Jessee, Ronald K. Esplin, and Richard

Lyman Bushman (Salt Lake City, UT: Church Historian's Press, 2009), 75, 77; Richard Lloyd Anderson, "I Have a Question," *Ensign,* January 1979, 13–14.

2. D&C 57.

3. *The Evening and the Morning Star,* June 1832–July 1833; Peter Crawley, *A Descriptive Bibliography of the Mormon Church, Volume One, 1830–1847* (Provo, UT: Religious Studies Center, Brigham Young University, 1997), 32–34. The very first article in the June 1832 issue is headed "Revelations."

4. James B. Allen and Glen M. Leonard, *The Story of the Latter-day Saints,* 2d ed. (Salt Lake City, UT: Deseret Book, 1992), 92–94.

5. "The Book of Mormon," *The Evening and the Morning Star,* June 1833.

6. Joseph Smith Jr., Sidney Rigdon, and F. G. Williams to W. W. Phelps and others, June 25, 1833, Joseph Smith Letter Book 1, p. 45, in Richard E. Turley Jr., ed., *Selected Collections from the Archives of The Church of Jesus Christ of Latter-day Saints* (Provo, UT: Brigham Young University Press, 2002), vol. 1, DVD 20; "History of Joseph Smith," *The Latter Day Saints' Millennial Star* 14, no. 29 (September 11, 1852): 449; "Letter to Brethren in Zion, June 25, 1833," in Joseph Smith, *History of the Church of Jesus Christ of Latter-day Saints,* 2d ed., ed. B. H. Roberts, 7 vols. (Salt Lake City, UT: Deseret Book, 1948–53), 1:363.

7. "The Book of Mormon," *The Evening and the Morning Star,* July 1833.

8. Allen and Leonard, *Story of the Latter-day Saints,* 94–96.

9. Milton V. Backman Jr., *The Heavens Resound: A History of the Latter-day Saints in Ohio, 1830–1838* (Salt Lake City, UT: Deseret Book, 1983), 155–56; Joseph Smith Jr., trans., The Book of Mormon, 2d ed. (Kirtland, OH: P. P. Pratt and J. Goodson, 1837), [v]; Crawley, *Descriptive Bibliography,* 1:66–68. Ownership of the O. Cowdery & Co. printing establishment passed from Cowdery to Joseph Smith and Sidney Rigdon by February 1, 1837. "Notice," *Latter Day Saints' Messenger and Advocate* 3 (February 1837): 458. By the end of April that year, it had been transferred to William Marks. *Latter Day Saints' Messenger and Advocate* 3 (April 1837): 496.

10. Royal Skousen, "Book of Mormon, editions of," in Dennis L. Largey, gen. ed., *Book of Mormon Reference Companion* (Salt Lake City, UT: Deseret Book, 2003), 112; Royal Skousen, "Book of Mormon, Manuscripts and Editions," in Arnold K. Garr, Donald Q. Cannon, and Richard O. Cowan, *Encyclopedia of Latter-day Saint History* (Salt Lake City, UT: Deseret Book, 2000), 121. See also Royal Skousen, *The Printer's Manuscript of the Book of Mormon, Part One* (Provo, UT: Foundation for Ancient Research and Mormon Studies, Brigham Young University, 2001), 4, 18–19; Crawley, *Descriptive*

Bibliography, 1:67; Boyd K. Packer, "We Believe All That God Has Revealed," *Ensign,* May 1974, 93–95.

11. D&C 21:1. D&C 1:24 declares that God speaks "unto my servants in their weakness, after the manner of their language"—one explanation that has been given for why revelations in the voice of God appeared in Joseph Smith's language. On changes in the second edition, see Crawley, *Descriptive Bibliography,* 1:67.

12. James B. Allen, Ronald K. Esplin, and David J. Whittaker, *Men with a Mission, 1837–1841: The Quorum of the Twelve Apostles in the British Isles* (Salt Lake City, UT: Deseret Book, 1992).

13. The Book of Mormon (1837), [v]–vi.

14. "The Book of Mormon," *The Evening and the Morning Star,* July 1833; Doctrine and Covenants of the Church of the Latter Day Saints (Kirtland, OH: F. G. Williams & Co., 1835); Book of Mormon (1837), [v].

15. "To the Reader," Book of Mormon (1837), 621.

16. Book of Mormon (1837), [v].

17. "To the Reader," Book of Mormon (1837), 621.

18. Allen, Esplin, and Whittaker, *Men with a Mission,* 25–26, 249n52; Crawley, *Descriptive Bibliography,* 1:67–68.

19. Backman, *Heavens Resound,* 310–41; Smith, *History of the Church,* 2:489; Allen, Esplin, and Whittaker, *Men with a Mission.*

20. Backman, *Heavens Resound,* 342–49. Charges ran both directions on who was responsible for the blaze. Crawley, *Descriptive Bibliography,* 1:20.

21. Hepzibah Richards to Willard Richards, January 18, 1838, Willard Richards Papers, Church History Library, Salt Lake City, Utah.

22. John Smith to George A. Smith, January 15–18, 1838, George A. Smith Papers, Church History Library.

23. In the Book of Mormon (1837), [v], Pratt and Goodson write that they "obtained leave to issue five thousand copies."

24. Crawley, *Descriptive Bibliography,* 1:67.

25. Book of Mormon (1837), vi.

26. "The Book of Mormon," *The Evening and the Morning Star,* June 1833.

Chapter Five: The Third Edition, 1840

1. Dean C. Jessee, ed., *The Papers of Joseph Smith,* vol. 2 (Salt Lake City, UT: Deseret Book, 1992), 211.

2. Peter Crawley, *A Descriptive Bibliography of the Mormon Church, Volume One, 1830–1847* (Provo, UT: Religious Studies Center, Brigham Young University, 1997), 13; Kyle R. Walker, "'As Fire Shut Up in My Bones': Ebenezer Robinson, Don Carlos Smith, and the 1840 Edition

of the Book of Mormon," *Journal of Mormon History* 36 (Winter 2010): 9; B. H. Roberts, *A Comprehensive History of The Church of Jesus Christ of Latter-day Saints,* 6 vols. (Provo, UT: Brigham Young University Press, 1965), 1:139–40, 506; 2:45n6.

3. Crawley, *Descriptive Bibliography,* 1:19–20.

4. Alexander L. Baugh, *A Call to Arms: The 1838 Mormon Defense of Northern Missouri* (Provo, UT: Joseph Fielding Smith Institute for Latter-day Saint History/BYU Studies, 2000), 115–34, 213–16.

5. Crawley, *Descriptive Bibliography,* 1:20; Joseph Smith, *History of the Church of Jesus Christ of Latter-day Saints,* 2d ed., ed. B. H. Roberts, 7 vols. (Salt Lake City, UT: Deseret Book, 1948–53), 4:398; Walker, "As Fire Shut Up in My Bones,'" 7.

6. James B. Allen and Glen M. Leonard, *The Story of the Latter-day Saints,* 2d ed. (Salt Lake City, UT: Deseret Book, 1992), 137–56.

7. Walker, "'As Fire Shut Up in My Bones,'" 1–11; Crawley, *Descriptive Bibliography,* 1:20, 91; Smith, *History of the Church,* 4:398.

8. *Times and Seasons* 1 (Dec. 1839): 25; Smith, *History of the Church,* 4:49. When Parley P. Pratt wrote from New York about publishing the Book of Mormon there, Hyrum Smith replied, "Not only is the city of New York destitute of this book, but there is truly a famine throughout the Union, and another large edition is certainly required." Smith, *History of the Church,* 4:47.

9. Walker, "'As Fire Shut Up in My Bones,'" 3.

10. "Wanted," *Times and Seasons* 1 (April 1840): 91.

11. "Wanted," *Times and Seasons* 1 (May 1840): 112

12. Crawley, *Descriptive Bibliography,* 1:129, 131; Walker, "'As Fire Shut Up in My Bones,'" 13.

13. Walker, "'As Fire Shut Up in My Bones,'" 14; Larry W. Draper, "Book of Mormon Editions," in M. Gerald Bradford and Alison V. Coutts, eds., *Uncovering the Original Text of the Book of Mormon* (Provo, UT: The Foundation for Ancient Research and Mormon Studies, Brigham Young University, 2002), 42–43.

14. Walker, "'As Fire Shut Up in My Bones,'" 13–14.

15. Walker, "'As Fire Shut Up in My Bones,'" 14.

16. Royal Skousen, "Book of Mormon, editions of," in Dennis L. Largey, gen. ed., *Book of Mormon Reference Companion* (Salt Lake City, UT: Deseret Book, 2003), 112; Royal Skousen, "Book of Mormon Editions (1830–1981)," in Daniel H. Ludlow, ed., *Encyclopedia of Mormonism,* 4 vols. (New York, NY: Macmillan, 1992), 1:175; Crawley, *Descriptive Bibliography,* 1:132; Walker, "'As Fire Shut Up in My Bones,'" 15.

17. Joseph Smith Jr., [trans.], The Book of Mormon (Palmyra, NY: E. B. Grandin, 1830), 117; Joseph Smith Jr., trans., The Book of Mormon, 2d ed. (Kirtland, OH: P. P. Pratt and J. Goodson, 1837), 125.

18. Joseph Smith Jr., trans., The Book of Mormon (Nauvoo, IL: Robinson and Smith, 1840), 115; George Horton, "Understanding Textual Changes in the Book of Mormon," *Ensign*, December 1983, 28. Since 1879, the changed verse has been 2 Nephi 30:6 in Latter-day Saint editions. Crawley, *Descriptive Bibliography*, 1:132.

19. 1 Samuel 16:7. Cf. Royal Skousen, *Analysis of Textual Variants of the Book of Mormon, Part Two, 2 Nephi 11–Mosiah 16* (Provo, UT: The Foundation for Ancient Research and Mormon Studies, 2006), 895–99, which concludes that the change was made "probably because of a perceived difficulty in allowing a change in skin color to apply to the descendants of the Nephites."

20. Joseph Smith Jr., trans., The Book of Mormon, 3d ed. (Nauvoo, IL: Robinson and Smith, 1840), [3].

21. Crawley, *Descriptive Bibliography*, 1:132; Walker, "'As Fire Shut Up in My Bones,'" 15, 18–20.

22. Walker, "'As Fire Shut Up in My Bones,'" 21–22. Apparently, at first Ebenezer didn't realize the firm had published a pamphlet by Sidney Rigdon that Ebenezer himself had promoted before leaving Nauvoo. "To the Public," *Times and Seasons* 1 (May 1840): 112; Crawley, *Descriptive Bibliography*, 1:103–4, 131; Walker, "'As Fire Shut Up in My Bones,'" 22.

23. Walker, "'As Fire Shut Up in My Bones,'" 22–23.

24. Walker, "'As Fire Shut Up in My Bones,'" 24.

25. "To the Saints Scattered Abroad," *Times and Seasons* 1 (July 1840): 144; "To the Saints Scattered Abroad," *Times and Seasons* 1 (Aug. 1840): 160.

26. "Books!!!" *Times and Seasons* 1 (July 1840): 140; Walker, "'As Fire Shut Up in My Bones,'" 25, 28–29.

27. "Books!!!" *Times and Seasons* 1 (July 1840):139–40.

28. "Report from the Presidency," *Times and Seasons* 1 (October 1840): 188; "The Saints in America," *Millennial Star* 1 (January 1841): 229; Smith, *History of the Church*, 4:214.

29. "Minutes of the General Conference," *Times and Seasons* 1 (October 1840): 186; Walker, "'As Fire Shut Up in My Bones,'" 29; Smith, *History of the Church*, 4:206.

30. Walker, "'As Fire Shut Up in My Bones,'" 29.

31. Crawley, *Descriptive Bibliography*, 1:131–32; Walker, "'As Fire Shut Up in My Bones,'" 33–34.

32. Crawley, *Descriptive Bibliography*, 1:21, 92, 132; Walker, "'As Fire Shut Up in My Bones,'" 33–36.

33. Joseph F. Smith, "The Original Manuscript of the Book of Mormon," *Improvement Era,* November 1899, 64; "Original Manuscript of the Book of Mormon," *Improvement Era,* March 1900, 389–90; Dean C. Jessee, "The Original Book of Mormon Manuscript," *Brigham Young University Studies* 10 (Spring 1970): 264; Royal Skousen, "Book of Mormon, manuscripts of," in Largey, *Book of Mormon Reference Companion,* 125; Royal Skousen, "Book of Mormon, Manuscripts and Editions," in Arnold K. Garr, Donald Q. Cannon, and Richard O. Cowan, *Encyclopedia of Latter-day Saint History* (Salt Lake City, UT: Deseret Book, 2000), 120.

34. Walker, "'As Fire Shut Up in My Bones,'" 39.

Chapter Six:
The First European Edition, 1841

1. D&C 118:4–5.

2. Joseph Smith, *History of the Church of Jesus Christ of Latter-day Saints,* 2d ed., ed. B. H. Roberts, 7 vols. (Salt Lake City, UT: Deseret Book, 1948–53), 3:307; "Theodore Turley's Memorandums," Historian's Office, Joseph Smith History Documents, Church History Library, Salt Lake City, Utah.

3. "At a council held at Far West, by the Twelve," Joseph Smith Letter Book 2, pp. 138–39, in Richard E. Turley Jr., ed., *Selected Collections from the Archives of The Church of Jesus Christ of Latter-day Saints* (Provo, UT: Brigham Young University Press, 2002), vol. 1, DVD 20; James B. Allen, Ronald K. Esplin, and David J. Whittaker, *Men with a Mission, 1837–1841: The Quorum of the Twelve Apostles in the British Isles* (Salt Lake City, UT: Deseret Book, 1992), 57–58; James B. Allen and Glen M. Leonard, *The Story of the Latter-day Saints,* 2d ed. (Salt Lake City, UT: Deseret Book, 1992), 160–61.

4. Allen, Esplin, and Whittaker, *Men with a Mission,* 58–83.

5. Peter Crawley, *Descriptive Bibliography of the Mormon Church, Volume One, 1830–1847* (Provo, UT: Religious Studies Center, Brigham Young University, 1997), 151.

6. Hyrum Smith to Parley P. Pratt, Dec. 22, 1839, in Smith, *History of the Church,* 4:47–48. Parley wrote that the Book of Mormon was "not to be had in this part of the vineyard for love or money. Hundreds are waiting in various parts here about but there is truly a famine in that respect." Parley P. Pratt to Joseph Smith, Nov. 22, 1839, quoted in Allen, Esplin, and Whittaker, *Men with a Mission,* 249n53.

7. Crawley, *Descriptive Bibliography,* 1:148. On February 8, 1841, Heber C. Kimball and Wilford Woodruff finally obtained the copyright for Joseph Smith at Stationers' Hall, London, after the first copies of the book came off the press. Allen, Esplin, and

Whittaker, *Men with a Mission,* 251, 297.

8. Allen, Esplin, and Whittaker, *Men with a Mission,* 135.

9. Orson Hyde and John E. Page to Joseph Smith, May 1, 1840, in Smith, *History of the Church,* 4:123–24; Joseph Smith Jr. to Orson Hyde and John E. Page, May 14, 1840, in Smith, *History of the Church,* 4:128–29; Allen, Esplin, and Whittaker, *Men with a Mission,* 245.

10. Allen, Esplin, and Whittaker, *Men with a Mission,* 249–50.

11. Brigham Young to Joseph Smith, May 7, 1840, in Smith, *History of the Church,* 4:126.

12. Allen, Esplin, and Whittaker, *Men with a Mission,* 149, 151.

13. Allen, Esplin, and Whittaker, *Men with a Mission,* 250–51, 386.

14. Allen, Esplin, and Whittaker, *Men with a Mission,* 251.

15. Brigham Young and Willard Richards to Joseph Smith, Sidney Rigdon, and Hyrum Smith, September 5, 1840, in Allen, Esplin, and Whittaker, *Men with a Mission,* 394–95.

16. Eliza R. Snow Smith, *Biography and Family Record of Lorenzo Snow* (Salt Lake City, UT: Deseret News, 1884), 46–51; Allen, Esplin, and Whittaker, *Men with a Mission,* 245–46; summary of Joseph Smith's July 19, 1840, answer to Brigham Young's letter, Joseph Smith Letter Book 2:153, in Richard E. Turley Jr., ed., *Selected Collections from the Archives of The Church of Jesus Christ of Latter-day Saints* (Provo, UT: Brigham Young University Press, 2002), vol. 1, DVD 20.

17. Brigham Young to Mary Ann Young, November 12, 1840, in Allen, Esplin, and Whittaker, *Men with a Mission,* 246.

18. Dean C. Jessee, ed., *Personal Writings of Joseph Smith,* rev. ed. (Salt Lake City, UT: Deseret Book; Provo, UT: Brigham Young University Press, 2002), 517–18.

19. "Book of Mormon," *Millennial Star* 1 (February 1841): 263–64.

20. Allen, Esplin, and Whittaker, *Men with a Mission,* 251.

21. Allen, Esplin, and Whittaker, *Men with a Mission,* 252n67.

22. It did not, however, sell as well as expected, perhaps because of the Saints' poverty and the poor's inability to read. Crawley, *Descriptive Bibliography,* 1:150; Young and Richards to Smith, Rigdon, and Smith, in Allen, Esplin, and Whittaker, *Men with a Mission,* 391.

23. Crawley, *Descriptive Bibliography,* 1:150–51. Some copies of the 1840 Nauvoo edition reprinted after the Liverpool edition included a slightly edited version of the same index. Crawley, *Descriptive Bibliography,* 1:132. Some copies of the 1830 Book of Mormon contain a two-column "References to the Book of

Mormon," but it was not an original part of the first edition, having been published around 1835 and glued into the books. Crawley, *Descriptive Bibliography,* 1:60.

24. Allen, Esplin, and Whittaker, *Men with a Mission,* 275.

25. Smith, *Biography and Family Record,* 63; Leonard J. Arrington, *Brigham Young: American Moses* (New York, NY: Alfred A. Knopf, 1985), 84, 95.

26. "British Saints Celebrate 150th Anniversary," *Ensign,* October 1987, 70–71. As this source explains, Queen Victoria's copy of the book was found in the Royal Library at Windsor Castle in 1987. That same year, Church representatives in England presented copies of the latest edition of the scriptures to aides of Queen Elizabeth II and Prime Minister Margaret Thatcher. Inscriptions on these copies paralleled the ones on those donated in 1841, with the names of the recipients on the front cover and "Presented by Ezra Taft Benson" on the back.

27. Eliza R. Snow, "Queen Victoria," *Times and Seasons* 5, no. 1 (1844): 398; "Queen Victoria," in Smith, *Biography and Family Record,* 63–64; "Queen Victoria," in Jill Mulvay Derr and Karen Lynn Davidson, eds., *Eliza R. Snow: The Complete Poetry* (Provo, UT: Brigham Young University Press; Salt Lake City: University of Utah Press, 2009), 269.

28. "British Saints Celebrate 150th Anniversary," 71; LeRoi C. Snow, "When Queen Victoria Received a Book of Mormon," *Improvement Era,* July 1937, 417.

29. Royal Skousen, "Book of Mormon Editions (1830–1981)," in Daniel H. Ludlow, ed., *Encyclopedia of Mormonism,* 4 vols. (New York: Macmillan, 1992), 1:175. The 1841 edition also introduced "a few accidental changes," as might be expected when a book is reset in type. Royal Skousen, "Book of Mormon, editions of," in Dennis L. Largey, gen. ed., *Book of Mormon Reference Companion* (Salt Lake City, UT: Deseret Book, 2003), 112. Royal Skousen, ed., *The Book of Mormon: The Earliest Text* (New Haven, CT: Yale University Press, 2009, 740, calls the 1841 edition "basically a resetting of the 1837 edition, though poorly executed."

30. Crawley, *Descriptive Bibliography,* 1:205, observes that the 1842 "edition" is "technically . . . a later impression—probably the fourth— from the stereotype plates of the third edition, with a reset title page," and "the last printing of the Book of Mormon in America by the Church until the Salt Lake City edition [or impression] of 1871."

31. Allen, Esplin, and Whittaker, *Men with a Mission,* 251; Crawley, *Descriptive Bibliography,* 1:132, 151; Skousen, *The Book of Mormon: The Earliest Text,* 744. Skousen, "Book of Mormon Editions," in Ludlow, *Encyclopedia of Mormonism,* 1:176, points out: "The Reorganized Church of Jesus Christ of Latter Day Saints

(RLDS) also has its own textual tradition. Prior to 1874, the RLDS used an edition of the Book of Mormon published by James O. Wright (1858, New York), basically a reprinting of the 1840 Nauvoo edition. The first and second RLDS editions (1874, Plano, Illinois; and 1892, Lamoni, Iowa) followed the 1840 text." See also Skousen, "Book of Mormon, editions of," in Largey, *Book of Mormon Reference Companion,* 113–14; Skousen, *The Book of Mormon: The Earliest Text,* 744.

Chapter Seven: Chapter and Verse

1. On the history of chapter and verse numbers in the Bible, see Walter F. Specht, "Chapter and Verse Divisions," in Bruce M. Metzger and Michael D. Coogan, *The Oxford Companion to the Bible* (New York: Oxford University Press, 1993), 105–7; S. L. Greenslade, *The Cambridge History of the Bible: The West from the Reformation to the Present Day* (Cambridge: Cambridge University Press, 1963), 62, 419–22, 436–37, 442–43.

2. Royal Skousen, ed., *The Book of Mormon: The Earliest Text* (New Haven, CT: Yale University Press, 2009), xl.

3. D&C 10:41; A Book of Commandments (Zion [Independence, MO]: W. W. Phelps & Co., 1833), 25; Royal Skousen, *The Printer's Manuscript of the Book of Mormon, Part One* (Provo, UT: The Foundation for Ancient Research and Mormon Studies, Brigham Young University, 2001), plate 3.

4. Skousen, *Printer's Manuscript of the Book of Mormon, Part One,* 41, plate 3, 284; Royal Skousen, "Book of Mormon, manuscripts of," in Dennis L. Largey, gen. ed., *Book of Mormon Reference Companion* (Salt Lake City, UT: Deseret Book, 2003), 124–25.

5. Cf. Joseph Smith Jr., [trans.], The Book of Mormon (Palmyra, NY: E. B. Grandin, 1830), 221–407, with Joseph Smith Jr., trans., The Book of Mormon (Salt Lake City, UT: The Church of Jesus Christ of Latter-day Saints, 1981), 207–368.

6. John H. Gilbert, *Recollections,* September 8, 1892, typescript, Harold B. Lee Library, Brigham Young University, Provo, UT; John H. Gilbert, *Recollections,* in Mark L. McConkie, *Remembering Joseph* (Salt Lake City, UT: Deseret Book, 2003), 234.

7. Skousen, *The Book of Mormon: The Earliest Text,* xliv; Royal Skousen, "Book of Mormon, Manuscripts and Editions," in Arnold K. Garr, Donald Q. Cannon, and Richard O. Cowan, *Encyclopedia of Latter-day Saint History* (Salt Lake City, UT: Deseret Book, 2000), 121.

8. Book of Mormon (1830), 56–59, 59–62, 202–5, 296–99, 301–4, 333–36, 337–40, 395–98, 438–41, 477–80, 485–88, 518–21, 552–55, 562–65, 585–88.

9. Book of Mormon (1830), 232–36, 445–49, 555–59, 567–71.

10. Book of Mormon (1830), 531–38.

11. Book of Mormon (1830), 139–40, 513–14, 574–76, 585–88.

12. Joseph Smith Jr., trans., The Book of Mormon (Kirtland, OH: P. P. Pratt and J. Goodson, 1837), 561–67; Joseph Smith Jr., trans., The Book of Mormon, 3d ed. (Nauvoo, IL: Robinson and Smith, 1840), 517–23; Joseph Smith Jr., trans., The Book of Mormon, 1st European ed. (Liverpool: J. Tompkins, 1841), 573–80; Joseph Smith, trans., The Book of Mormon, 4th American ed. (Nauvoo, IL: Joseph Smith, 1842), 517–23; Joseph Smith Jr., trans., The Book of Mormon, 2d European ed. (Liverpool: Orson Pratt, 1849), 509–15.

13. Joseph Smith Jr., trans., The Book of Mormon, 3d European ed. (Liverpool: F. D. Richards, 1852).

14. Book of Mormon (1852).

15. The Book of Mormon, electrotype ed. (Liverpool: William Budge, 1879); Royal Skousen, "Book of Mormon, editions of," in Largey, *Book of Mormon Reference Companion*, 112–13.

16. Book of Mormon (1852), 509–15; Book of Mormon (1879), 563–69.

17. Skousen, *The Book of Mormon: The Earliest Text*, 740; Skousen, "Book of Mormon, editions of," in Largey, *Book of Mormon Reference Companion*, 112–13. As Skousen points out, the Community of Christ, formerly the Reorganized Church of Jesus Christ of Latter Day Saints, continues to use the original large chapter numbers.

Chapter Eight: The 1920 Edition

1. Royal Skousen, "Book of Mormon, editions of," in Dennis L. Largey, gen. ed., *Book of Mormon Reference Companion* (Salt Lake City, UT: Deseret Book, 2003), 113.

2. Joseph Smith Jr., [trans.], The Book of Mormon (Palmyra, NY: E. B. Grandin, 1830), 5, 59, 452, 514. The manuscripts were even more confusing since the first two books were originally both called the same thing: "The Book of Nephi." Later, Oliver Cowdery added the words "first" and "second" to distinguish the two. Royal Skousen, *The Original Manuscript of the Book of Mormon* (Provo, UT: Foundation for Ancient Research and Mormon Studies, Brigham Young University, 2001), 164; Royal Skousen, *The Printer's Manuscript of the Book of Mormon, Part One* (Provo, UT: Foundation for Ancient Research and Mormon Studies, Brigham Young University, 2001), 52, 143; Royal Skousen, ed., *The Book of Mormon: The Earliest Text* (New Haven, CT: Yale University Press, 2009), 745, 752. The "First Book of Nephi" was subtitled "His Reign and Ministry" in the first edition and subsequent Latter-day Saint editions. Punctuation in the titles of the books has varied over time.

3. Joseph Smith Jr., trans., *The Book of Mormon* (Kirtland, OH: P. P. Pratt and J. Goodson, 1837), 477, 542.

4. Joseph Smith Jr., trans., *The Book of Mormon*, electrotype ed. (Liverpool: William Budge, 1879), 475, 543.

5. Deseret Sunday School Union editions took this approach. See, e.g., Joseph Smith Jr., trans., *The Book of Mormon* (Salt Lake City, UT: Deseret Sunday School Union, 1908), 498, 570.

6. Joseph Smith Jr., trans., *The Book of Mormon* (Salt Lake City, UT: The Church of Jesus Christ of Latter-day Saints, 1920), 399, 456. In the title of Fourth Nephi, the 1920 edition also added a dash between the second instance of "Nephi" and "One of the Disciples of Jesus Christ."

7. Skousen, *The Book of Mormon: The Earliest Text,* 741.

8. See, e.g., S. L. Greenslade, *The Cambridge History of the Bible: The West from the Reformation to the Present Day* (Cambridge: Cambridge University Press, 1963), plates between pp. 56 and 57, especially plates 1 and 38.

9. Skousen, "Book of Mormon, editions of," in Largey, *Book of Mormon Reference Companion,* 113.

10. On styles of the triple combination scriptures (Book of Mormon, Doctrine and Covenants, and Pearl of Great Price), see Heber J. Grant, Charles W. Penrose, and Anthony W. Ivins, "Official Announcement," in James R. Clark, ed., *Messages of the First Presidency of The Church of Jesus Christ of Latter-day Saints,* vol. 5 (Salt Lake City, UT: Bookcraft, 1971), 207–8. Examples of matching leather sets—Bibles and triple combination scriptures—are found in the collections of the Church History Library, Salt Lake City, Utah.

11. Skousen, *Printer's Manuscript of the Book of Mormon, Part One,* 30; Skousen, *Original Manuscript of the Book of Mormon,* 8, 25, and plates 5–7, 9.

12. Skousen, *Original Manuscript of the Book of Mormon,* 164. Summaries that were part of the earliest text include those before the books of 1 Nephi, 2 Nephi, Jacob, Alma, Helaman, 3 Nephi, and 4 Nephi. Skousen, *Original Manuscript of the Book of Mormon,* 164, 487, 512; Skousen, *Printer's Manuscript of the Book of Mormon, Part One,* 52, 143, 240, 389; Royal Skousen, *The Printer's Manuscript of the Book of Mormon, Part Two* (Provo, UT: Foundation for Ancient Research and Mormon Studies, Brigham Young University, 2001), 710–11, 777, 870. A summary may also have been given for the book of Mosiah. If so, it was with the 116 pages lost by Martin Harris. See Skousen, *Printer's Manuscript of the Book of Mormon, Part One,* Plate 3. In 1920, a summary was also added to the beginning of the Book of Ether. Skousen, *The Book of Mormon: The Earliest Text,* 786. Nearly all the headings have been edited slightly for

publication since their original dictation.

13. Skousen, *Printer's Manuscript of the Book of Mormon, Part One,* 356. Other examples include the summaries between the following current chapters: Mosiah 8 and 9; Alma 4 and 5, 6 and 7, 8 and 9, 16 and 17, 20 and 21, 35 and 36, 37 and 38, 38 and 39, 44 and 45; Helaman 6 and 7, 12 and 13; 3 Nephi 10 and 11. Skousen, *Original Manuscript of the Book of Mormon,* 319, 335, 339, 372; Skousen, *Printer's Manuscript of the Book of Mormon, Part One,* 314, 408, 420, 430, 471; Skousen, *Printer's Manuscript of the Book of Mormon, Part Two,* 498, 572, 583, 585, 611, 739, 761, 810.

14. Book of Mormon (1920), 523–30.

15. Book of Mormon (1920), 531–34.

16. Paul Y. Hoskisson, "Names in the Book of Mormon," in Largey, *Book of Mormon Reference Companion,* 580.

17. Mary Jane Woodger, "How the Guide to English Pronunciation of Book of Mormon Names Came About," *Journal of Book of Mormon Studies* 9, no. 1 (2000): 54–55.

18. Woodger, "How the Guide," 55; George Reynolds, *A Dictionary of the Book of Mormon* (Salt Lake City, UT: Deseret Sunday School Union, 1910), 353–63.

19. Heber J. Grant to Reed Smoot, October 12, 1921, in Clark, *Messages of the First Presidency,* 206.

20. *2010 Church Almanac* (Salt Lake City, UT: Deseret News, 2009), 91.

21. "Conference Address of President Anthony W. Ivins," *Liahona: The Elders' Journal* 19, no. 1 (July 5, 1921): 2–3.

Chapter Nine: The 1981 Edition

1. Royal Skousen, *The Book of Mormon: The Earliest Text* (New Haven, CT: Yale University Press, 2009), 741, 743–44.

2. "Scriptures: 'a welcome oasis to weary traveler,'" *Church News,* September 25, 1999. Many examples of these Bibles can be found in the collections of the Church History Library, Salt Lake City, Utah.

3. *That Promised Day: The Coming Forth of the LDS Scriptures* (Provo, UT: BYU Broadcasting and Martin Andersen Productions, LLC, 2010). This video production ran between sessions of the Church's general conference on October 3, 2010. Daniel H. Ludlow, "Correlation," in Arnold K. Garr, Donald Q. Cannon, and Richard O. Cowan, *Encyclopedia of Latter-day Saint History* (Salt Lake City, UT: Deseret Book, 2000), 250–51; Frank O. May Jr., "Correlation of the Church, Administration," in Daniel H. Ludlow, ed., *Encyclopedia of Mormonism,* 4 vols. (New York: Macmillan, 1992), 1:323–25; "Scriptures: 'a welcome oasis to weary traveler.'"

4. *That Promised Day;* Heidi S. Swinton, *To the Rescue: The Biography of Thomas S. Monson* (Salt Lake City, UT:

Deseret Book, 2010), 368–70; Boyd K. Packer, "Scriptures," *Ensign,* November 1982, 51–53; Lucile C. Tate, *Boyd K. Packer: A Watchman on the Tower* (Salt Lake City, UT: Bookcraft, 1995), 213–20; Joseph Fielding McConkie, *The Bruce R. McConkie Story* (Salt Lake City, UT: Deseret Book, 2003), 381–82; Dennis B. Horne, *Bruce R. McConkie* (Roy, UT: Eborn Books, 2000), 188–89; Robert J. Matthews, "'A Bible! A Bible!'" *Ensign,* January 1987, 27; "Scriptures: 'a welcome oasis to weary traveler'"; Bruce T. Harper, "The Church Publishes a New Triple Combination," *Ensign,* October 1981, 9–10.

5. *That Promised Day;* Swinton, *To the Rescue,* 369; Tate, *Boyd K. Packer,* 213. Elder Marvin J. Ashton served as a member of the Bible Study Aids Committee that became the Scriptures Publication Committee but was later called to another assignment and replaced by Elder McConkie.

6. *That Promised Day;* Swinton, *To the Rescue,* 368–69, 387–88; Boyd K. Packer, "The Library of the Lord," *Ensign,* May 1990, 36; "Scriptures: 'a welcome oasis to weary traveler.'"

7. *That Promised Day;* Swinton, *To the Rescue,* 386–87; Tate, *Boyd K. Packer,* 215–16.

8. *That Promised Day;* Swinton, *To the Rescue,* 387; Tate, *Boyd K. Packer,* 214–15.

9. *That Promised Day;* Swinton, *To the Rescue,* 387; Tate, *Boyd K. Packer,* 215, 222; McConkie, *Bruce R. McConkie Story,* 347, 381–84, 427–28; Horne, *Bruce R. McConkie,* 191–93.

10. Joseph Smith Jr., trans., The Book of Mormon (Salt Lake City: The Church of Jesus Christ of Latter-day Saints, 1981), [iii].

11. Book of Mormon (1981), [iv–vii]; Joseph Smith Jr., trans., The Book of Mormon (Salt Lake City, UT: The Church of Jesus Christ of Latter-day Saints, 1920), [iv–vi]; Royal Skousen, "Book of Mormon, editions of," in Dennis L. Largey, gen. ed., *Book of Mormon Reference Companion* (Salt Lake City, UT: Deseret Book, 2003), 113.

12. Book of Mormon (1920), [iii]; Book of Mormon (1981), [viii].

13. Harper, "Church Publishes a New Triple Combination," 10–11.

14. Cf. Book of Mormon (1920), 523–30, to Book of Mormon (1981).

15. Harper, "Church Publishes a New Triple Combination," 11–13.

16. Harper, "Church Publishes a New Triple Combination," 11–14.

17. Dean C. Jessee, "The Original Book of Mormon Manuscript," *BYU Studies* 10 (Spring 1970): 259–78.

18. Ronald E. Romig, "Elizabeth Ann Whitmer Cowdery: A Historical Reflection of Her Life," in Alexander L. Baugh, ed., *Days Never to Be Forgotten: Oliver Cowdery* (Provo, UT: Religious Studies Center, Brigham Young University, 2009), 327–38.

19. "Church Acquires Historical Documents," *Ensign,* June 1975, 34.

20. Royal Skousen, "Book of Mormon Editions (1830–1981)," in Ludlow, *Encyclopedia of Mormonism,* 1:176; Skousen, "Book of Mormon, editions of," in Largey, *Book of Mormon Reference Companion,* 113.

21. Joseph Smith Jr., [trans.], The Book of Mormon (Palmyra, NY: E. B. Grandin, 1830), 117; Joseph Smith Jr., trans., The Book of Mormon, 2d ed. (Kirtland, OH: P. P. Pratt and J. Goodson, 1837), 125; Joseph Smith Jr., trans., The Book of Mormon, 3d ed. (Nauvoo, IL: Robinson and Smith, 1840), 115; George Horton, "Understanding Textual Changes in the Book of Mormon," *Ensign,* December 1983, 27–28; Harper, "Church Publishes a New Triple Combination," 18; Skousen, *The Book of Mormon: The Earliest Text,* 754. Since 1879, the changed verse has been 2 Nephi 30:6 in Latter-day Saint editions.

22. Horton, "Understanding Textual Changes," 28; Skousen, *The Book of Mormon: The Earliest Text,* 743, 754.

23. Harper, "Church Publishes a New Triple Combination," 17–19; Horton, "Understanding Textual Changes," 27–28.

24. Book of Mormon (1981), [viii].

25. Ezekiel 37:19.

26. The Holy Bible (Salt Lake City, UT: The Church of Jesus Christ of Latter-day Saints, 1979), 1079, headnote to Ezekiel 37.

27. Harper, "Church Publishes a New Triple Combination," 10–14.

28. "New Triple Combination," *Ensign,* October 1981, 81, notes that "the feasibility of publishing a new 'quadruple combination' (binding together the Bible and the triple combination) is being studied." Quadruple combination scriptures had been published for decades, but without the integrated cross-referencing of the 1979 Bible edition and the 1981 editions of the Book of Mormon, Doctrine and Covenants, and Pearl of Great Price.

29. Packer, "Library of the Lord," 36.

30. Packer, "Scriptures," 53; Skousen, *The Book of Mormon: The Earliest Text,* 745.

31. Packer, "Scriptures," 53.

Chapter Ten: "The Keystone of Our Religion"

1. See pp. 27–37 herein.

2. See pp. 38–51 herein.

3. See pp. 52–65 herein.

4. See pp. 66–79 herein.

5. See pp. 80–91 herein.

6. See pp. 92–105 herein.

7. See pp. 106–115 herein.

8. See p. 114 herein.

9. Joseph Smith, *History of the Church of Jesus Christ of Latter-day Saints,* 2d ed., ed. B. H. Roberts, 7 vols.

(Salt Lake City, UT: Deseret Book, 1948–53), 4:461; Wilford Woodruff Journal, November 28, 1841, Church History Library, Salt Lake City, Utah. See also Scott C. Esplin, "Getting 'Nearer to God': A History of Joseph Smith's Statement," in *Living the Book of Mormon: Abiding by Its Precepts,* ed. Gaye Strathearn and Charles Swift (Provo, UT: Religious Studies Center, Brigham Young University; Salt Lake City: Deseret Book, 2007), 41–54.

10. By "correct," Joseph was undoubtedly referring to the book's doctrine, not its printing. Still, corrections to the text, even in printings since 1981, have improved how the doctrine is presented.

11. Joseph Smith Jr., trans., The Book of Mormon (Salt Lake City, UT: The Church of Jesus Christ of Latter-day Saints, 1981), [i].

12. "Yea, come unto Christ, and be perfected in him" (Moroni 10:32).

13. Cf., e.g., Joseph Smith Jr., [trans.], The Book of Mormon (Palmyra, NY: E. B. Grandin, 1830), 589–90, and Joseph Smith Jr., trans., The Book of Mormon (Salt Lake City, UT: The Church of Jesus Christ of Latter-day Saints, 1981), [iv]. The 1841 first European edition was the first edition of the Book of Mormon to have the witnesses' testimony at the front of the book. Peter Crawley, *A Descriptive Bibliography of the Mormon Church, Volume One, 1830–1847* (Provo, UT: Religious Studies Center, Brigham Young University, 1997), 151.

14. "The Testimony of Eight Witnesses," in Book of Mormon (1981), [iv]. The eight men were Christian Whitmer, Jacob Whitmer, Peter Whitmer Jr., John Whitmer, Hiram Page, Joseph Smith Sr., Hyrum Smith, and Samuel H. Smith.

15. "The Testimony of Three Witnesses," in Book of Mormon (1981), [iv].

16. Glen M. Leonard, *Nauvoo: A Place of Peace, A People of Promise* (Salt Lake City, UT: Deseret Book; Provo, UT: Brigham Young University Press, 2002), 374–76, 573–76; Smith, *History of the Church,* 6:547.

17. Smith, *History of the Church,* 6:545–49.

18. Leonard, *Nauvoo,* 369–71, 376–84.

19. D&C 135:4; Joseph Smith, The Doctrine and Covenants of The Church of Jesus Christ of Latter Day Saints, 2d ed. (Nauvoo, IL: John Taylor, 1844), 444–45.

20. D&C 135:5, quoting Ether 12:36, which, before the 1879 edition divided the book into smaller chapters and numbered verses, was near the end of Ether 5. See Doctrine and Covenants (1844), 445.

21. Leonard, *Nauvoo,* 387–98.

22. D&C 135:6; Doctrine and Covenants (1844), 445.

23. Book of Mormon (1981), [iii].

24. Moroni 10:32; Omni 1:26.

25. JS-H 1:60.

26. Moroni 10:27, 29, 34.

Index

Page numbers in italics indicate photographs and other illustrations.

1830 edition of the Book of Mormon. *See* First edition of the Book of Mormon.
1837 edition of the Book of Mormon. *See* Second edition of the Book of Mormon.
1840 edition of the Book of Mormon. *See* Third edition of the Book of Mormon.
1841 edition of the Book of Mormon. *See* First European edition of the Book of Mormon.
1852 edition of the Book of Mormon. *See* Third European edition of the Book of Mormon.
1879 edition of the Book of Mormon. *See* Electrotype edition of the Book of Mormon.
1920 edition of the Book of Mormon: modifications in, 93–100; columns in, *97*; chapter summaries in, *101*; "Synopsis of Chapters" in, *102*; "Pronouncing Vocabulary" in, *103*; title page of, *104*; publication of, 105; chapter headnotes and footnotes in, *110*
1981 edition of the Book of Mormon: Scriptures Publication Committee and, 107–8; modifications in, 109–13; chapter headnotes and footnotes in, *111*; Topical Guide in, 114

Albert, Prince, 77
Ammaron, xi–xii
Anthon, Charles, 13
Apostasy of 1837 and 1838, 53

Ballard, Melvin J., 93, *95*
Bible, *98*, 99, 107–9, 113–14, *115*
Books of Nephi, 93–99
Brother of Jared, 8

Carthage, Illinois, 122
Chapters and verses, addition of, 81–85
Chapter summaries, 99–100, *101*, 109. *See also* "Synopsis of Chapters"
Church Administration Building, *92*
Church Office Building, *106*
Church of Jesus Christ of Latter-day Saints, The, organization of, 39
Cincinnati, Ohio, *52*, 57–61
Cole, Abner, 32–36
Coleridge, Samuel Taylor, vii
Columns, 99

Conference Center, *116*
Copyright, to Book of Mormon, 27, *28*, 32–36, 71
Cowdery, Oliver: as scribe, 19–20; as witness, 20–23, *22*, 121; handwriting of, *21*; first edition and, 29, 30, 112; copyright infringement and, 32; second edition and, 43; excommunication of, 53; chapter breaks and, 81–82
Crucifixion, 8
Cumorah, xiv, *xvi*, 1–3

Deseret Sunday School Union Board, 100
Doctrine and Covenants, 44, 47
Double-column format, 99

Eight Witnesses, 23
Electrotype edition of the Book of Mormon (1879), 85, *91*, *96*
England, Twelve called to, 67
The Evening and the Morning Star, 39–40, *41*

Far West, Missouri, 53, 67, *68*
First edition of the Book of Mormon (1830): preface to, *24–25*; publication of, 27–36; original uncut sheet from, *34–35*; title page of, *37*; second edition and, *51*; change to, *59*; manuscript for, 62, 112; chapters and verses in, 81–82; pages from, *87–88*
First European edition of the Book of Mormon (1841): events preceding, 67–71; publication of, 72–74; bindings of, *75*; influence of, 77–78
Footnotes, 109, *110*, *111*

Gadianton robbers, xi, xiii
Gilbert, John, 31, *31*, 82
Golden plates: retrieved from Hill Cumorah, 1–3; description of, 3–7; contents of, 8; testify of Jesus Christ, 9–10; returned to Moroni, 23
Goodson, John, 43, 44, 47, 48
Grandin, Egbert B., 27, 29–32, *29*
Grandin's print shop, *26*, 27

Harmony, Pennsylvania: Smith home in, *12*; Joseph and Emma move to, 13
Harris, Martin, *18*; as witness, 4, 20–23, *22*, 121; has characters translated, 13; lost Book of Mormon pages and, 14, 16–19; publication of first edition and, 29–30, 31, 36; chapter breaks and, 81
Haun's Mill massacre, 53, *54*
Hebrew, 7
Herefordshire Beacon, *66*, 71
Hill Cumorah, xiv, *xvi*, 1–3
Howard, Luther, 27, 30, 36

Independence, Missouri, 39–43
Interpreter stones. *See* Urim and Thummim
Ivins, Anthony W., 93, *95*, 105

Jaredites, xiv, 8
Jesus Christ, Book of Mormon as testament of, 9–10, 114
John Tompkins & Company, 72, 74
Joseph, stick of, 113, 114
Judah, stick of, 113, 114

Kimball, Heber C., 77
King James Version, 107–9, *115*
Kirtland, Ohio, 47–48
Kirtland Temple, *38*

Lakey, Thomas, 36
Liverpool, England, *80*
Lost pages, of Book of Mormon, 14–19, 24–25, 81

Malvern Hills, England, *66*, 71
Manchester, New York, Smith home in, *17*
Martyrdom, 78, 121–25
McConkie, Bruce R., 108
Millennial Star, 74
Missionary work, 44, 67
Monson, Thomas S., 108
Moriancumer (brother of Jared), *6*, 8
Mormon, *x*, xii–xiv, 8
Mormon Missouri War, 53
Moroni, xiv–xv, *xv*, 1–3, 8, 9, 126

INDEX

Nauvoo, Illinois, 54–57, *55*
Nauvoo House cornerstone, 62, *63*, 112
Nephi, books of, 93–99

Original manuscript, *21*, 62, 112

Packer, Boyd K., 108, 114
Page, Hiram, 23
Palmyra, New York, *26*, 29
Phelps, William W., 39–40, *42*, 44, 51, 53
Pratt, Orson, 85
Pratt, Parley P., 43–44, 47–48, 68, *69*, 71
Printing press, *49*, 53, 54
Print shop, destruction of, 40–43, 47–48
"Pronouncing Vocabulary," 100, *103*
Publication of the Book of Mormon: first edition, 27–36; second edition, 39–51; third edition, 53–65; first European edition, 72–74; 1920 edition, 105

Quadruple combination, 113

The Reflector, 32–36, *33*
Reorganized Church of Jesus Christ of Latter Day Saints, 112
Revelation: translation through, 14; for Martin Harris, 36; on Independence, Missouri, 39; given to Ebenezer Robinson, 57; on missionary work, 67
Reynolds, George, 100
Richards, Franklin D., 82–85, *83*
Richards, George F., 93, *95*
Richards, Hepzibah, 47–48
Richards, Willard, *46*, 47–48
Robinson, Ebenezer, 54, *56*, 57–61, 62–65
Rochester, New York, 29

Scriptures Publication Committee, 108
Second edition of the Book of Mormon (1837): publication of, 39–51; printer's manuscript of, *45*; title page of, *50*; first edition and, *51*; change to, *59*
Seer stone, 13. *See also* Urim and Thummim
Shepard, Edward, 58–61, 62–65
Smith, Don Carlos, 54, 57, 61–62

Smith, Emma, 3, 4, *5*, *12*, 14–15
Smith, Hyrum: lost Book of Mormon pages and, 16; as witness, 23; first edition and, 29, 30, 31; copyright infringement and, 32; first European edition and, 68–71; martyrdom of, 121–25; Book of Mormon of, *123*; with Joseph Smith, *124*
Smith, Joseph: retrieves golden plates, 1–3; on golden plates' appearance, 3–4; on golden plates' title page, 7; receives Urim and Thummim, 9; home of, *12*; translates Book of Mormon, 13–14, 19–20; loses newborn child, 14–15, *15*; lost Book of Mormon pages and, 15–19, *24–25*; returns golden plates, 23; first edition and, 27–30; copyright infringement and, 32; second edition and, 43–44; leaves Kirtland, 47; in Far West, Missouri, 53; third edition and, 58; calls Twelve to English mission, 67; first European edition and, 71, 72–73; martyrdom of, 78, 121–25; chapter breaks and, 81, 82; on Book of Mormon, 118; with Hyrum Smith, *124*
Smith, Joseph F., 100
Smith, Joseph Fielding, 93, *95*
Smith, Joseph Sr., 16, *17*, 23, 32
Smith, Lucy Mack, 16, *17*, 19, 23, 30
Smith, Samuel, 19, 23
Snow, Eliza R., 77–78
Snow, Lorenzo, 72, *76*, 77
Stereotype/Stereotyping, 57, 58
Stick of Joseph, 113, 114
Stick of Judah, 113, 114
Stones, interpreter. *See* Urim and Thummim
"Synopsis of Chapters," 100, *102*, 109

Talmage, James E., 93, *95*
Taylor, John, 122–25
Third edition of the Book of Mormon (1840), 65; publication of, 53–65; change to, *59*; title page of, *60*, *64*
Third European edition of the Book of Mormon (1852), 82–85, *84, 89–90*

Three Witnesses, of Book of Mormon, 20, *22*, 118–21, *120*
Times and Seasons, 54, 57, 61–62
Tompkins, John, 72, 74
Topical Guide, 114
Translation, of Book of Mormon, 13–14, 19–20
Twelve Apostles, called to English mission, 67–71

Urim and Thummim, xiv, 8, 9, 13

Verses, addition of chapters and, 81–85
Victoria, Queen, 77–78, *79*

Wayne Sentinel, 36
Wheatley, Sir Henry, 77

Whitmer, David: on golden plates, 4; Book of Mormon translation and, 20; as witness, 20–23, *22*, 121; Book of Mormon manuscript and, 112
Whitmer, John, 23
Whitmer, Mary, 20, 39
Whitmer, Peter, 20, 39
Whitmer, Peter Jr., 23
Witnesses, of Book of Mormon, 20–23, *22*, 118–21, *120*, 125–26
Woodruff, Wilford, *119*

Young, Brigham, 67, *70*, 71–73, 77
Young, Mary Ann, 73, *73*

Zarahemla, xii
Zion, 39